The Future of Food Manufacturing

A Guide to Innovation, Sustainability, and Resilience

ERIC COMINSKI JR.

Copyright © 2024 Eric Cominski Jr.

All rights reserved. This book or any portion thereof may not be reproduced or used in any manner whatsoever without the express written permission of the publisher except for the use of brief quotations in a book review.

From Personal Growth to Shared Knowledge

This book wouldn't be here without the incredible support of many people. I embarked on a journey of self-development, aiming to become a valuable asset within my company in the food service and food manufacturing industry.

During this process, I observed a crucial gap in understanding how different aspects of the business interweave to create success. It wasn't just about individual growth, but about recognizing the interconnectedness of every role.

Inspired by this realization, I discovered a powerful link within the industry, where each piece plays a vital role in the bigger picture. This book serves as a tool and resource, bridging that very gap for those seeking to enhance their self-development and gain a holistic understanding of how everything works together.

Special Thanks

I want to thank everyone that took the time to give me feedback (good or bad) and took the time to listen to what I had to say.

A Shared Success

My hope is that this book empowers you to achieve both personal and professional growth, just as it has for me. Thank you for being a part of this journey.

Table of Contents

Chapter 1	The Food Manufacturing Ecosystem - A Symphony of Roles	1
Chapter 2	Cultivating a Thriving Workforce: Building Skills for Success	19
Chapter 3	Ensuring the Highest Standards of Safety and Quality: A Top Priority	39
Chapter 4	Leading from the Front: Strategies for Supervisors	53
Chapter 5	Optimizing Operations for Non-Frontline Workers	69
Chapter 6	Continuous Learning: A Key to Growth	79
Chapter 7	Building Your Value Proposition: Attracting and Retaining Top Talent	87
Chapter 8	Embracing Technological Advancements: The Future of Food Manufacturing	97
Chapter 9	Sustainability in Food Manufacturing: Balancing Growth with Responsibility	103
Chapter 10	Building a Resilient Food Manufacturing Workforce: Navigating Change and Ensuring Continuity	111
Chapter 11	The Future of Food Manufacturing: A Tapestry of Innovation, Sustainability, and Resilience	121
Chapter 12	A Roadmap for Success: Putting the Pieces Together	127
	Resources	135

CHAPTER 1

The Food Manufacturing Ecosystem - A Symphony of Roles

The journey from farm to table is a complex dance, with countless individuals playing critical roles in ensuring safe, high-quality food reaches consumers. This intricate network, known as the food manufacturing ecosystem, thrives on the interconnectedness of its various departments and the dedication of its workforce.

According to the World Bank, the global food processing industry is valued at over $13 trillion, making it a vital sector of the global economy.

This chapter delves into the fascinating world of food manufacturing, unveiling its intricacies and introducing the diverse cast of characters who make it all happen. We'll explore the roles and responsibilities of frontline workers, supervisors, managers, and executives, highlighting how each piece contributes to the final symphony of a successful food manufacturing company.

The Production Floor: Where the Magic Happens

Imagine a bustling production floor, a hive of activity driven by the tireless efforts of frontline workers. These individuals are the backbone of the food manufacturing ecosystem. Their responsibilities are as diverse as the products they create, ranging from operating complex machinery and packaging lines to conducting quality checks and ensuring sanitation protocols are followed meticulously.

- **Machine Operators:** These skilled individuals are responsible for operating various equipment used throughout the production process. They ensure machines run smoothly, monitor performance metrics, and adjust settings as needed. From mixing ingredients to filling containers, their precise actions translate recipes into reality.

- **Line Workers:** These team members keep the production line flowing efficiently. They perform tasks like assembling packaging materials, loading ingredients, and inspecting finished products. Their vigilance and attention to detail are crucial for maintaining consistent quality control.

- **Sanitation Technicians:** Food safety is paramount. Sanitation technicians play a vital role in maintaining a clean and hygienic environment. They perform regular cleaning and disinfection procedures, ensuring the production floor adheres to strict regulations.

- **Maintenance Technicians:** Uptime is everything in manufacturing. These technicians ensure equipment is well-maintained and functions optimally. They conduct preventive maintenance checks, troubleshoot problems, and perform repairs to minimize downtime and keep production lines running smoothly.

These are just a few examples of the frontline heroes who are the foundation of food manufacturing. Their dedication, skill, and hard work are essential for producing the food that nourishes communities around the globe.

Beyond the Line: The Support System

The production floor is just one piece of the puzzle. A robust support system ensures everything runs smoothly and efficiently. Here, we meet the supervisors, managers, and executives who play critical roles in orchestrating the food manufacturing symphony.

- **Supervisors:** They are the bridge between frontline workers and management. Supervisors directly oversee production processes, providing guidance and support to their teams. They ensure adherence to safety protocols, quality standards, and production schedules. They are also responsible for identifying and addressing any challenges faced by frontline workers.

- **Production Managers:** They oversee the overall production process, ensuring it meets established goals and objectives. Production managers work closely with supervisors, scheduling production runs, allocating resources, and monitoring production efficiency. They analyze data to identify areas for improvement and implement changes to optimize processes.

- **Quality Control Specialists:** Food safety is a top priority. These specialists ensure strict adherence to regulations throughout the production process. They conduct inspections, analyze samples, and monitor critical control points to guarantee food quality and safety.

- **Supply Chain Managers:** They oversee the flow of raw materials and finished products. These individuals work with suppliers and logistics companies to ensure timely deliveries and minimize disruptions. In today's globalized world, their role is crucial for maintaining consistent production and inventory levels.

- **Engineering Teams:** They are responsible for maintaining and improving production equipment. Engineers develop and implement preventive maintenance plans, troubleshoot issues, and design modifications to enhance efficiency and productivity.

- **Human Resources (HR):** HR is responsible for attracting, hiring, and retaining a talented workforce. They develop training programs, handle employee relations, and ensure a safe and positive work environment.

Nestle: A Commitment to Quality Control

Nestlé, a global leader in food manufacturing, exemplifies a commitment to rigorous quality control measures throughout their production processes. Their multi-layered approach ensures the safety and quality of their products at every stage, from farm to fork.

Here's a glimpse into Nestle's quality control practices:

- **Stringent Supplier Standards:** Nestle establishes strict quality standards for their suppliers and works closely with them to ensure adherence to these guidelines. This proactive approach minimizes the risk of contamination or inconsistencies in raw materials.

- **In-House and Third-Party Testing:** Nestle utilizes a comprehensive testing program that involves both in-house laboratories and independent third-party testing facilities. This ensures a multi-faceted approach to quality control, leaving no room for error.

- **Advanced Quality Management Systems:** Nestle implements robust quality management systems across their global operations. These systems are based on internationally recognized standards like HACCP (Hazard Analysis and Critical Control Points) and ISO

(International Organization for Standardization) certifications, ensuring consistent quality control practices across all their facilities.

- **Continuous Improvement:** Nestle fosters a culture of continuous improvement within their quality control processes. They constantly evaluate and refine their methods to stay ahead of emerging challenges and ensure their products meet the highest safety standards.

By prioritizing quality control through these measures, Nestle demonstrates its dedication to consumer safety and trust. Their commitment to excellence serves as a benchmark for other companies within the food manufacturing industry.

Executives set the strategic direction for the company, overseeing all aspects of the food manufacturing ecosystem. They make critical decisions regarding production goals, resource allocation, and market expansion.

The Interconnected Web: How Each Role Contributes to the Final Product

The success of any food manufacturing company hinges on the seamless collaboration between all these roles. Imagine a complex recipe – each ingredient plays a specific role, and when combined in the right proportions, they create a delectable dish. Similarly, in food manufacturing, every department and individual contribute a unique element that ultimately leads to the creation of safe, high-quality food products.

- **Frontline workers** are the hands that execute the recipe, ensuring precise measurements and following procedures meticulously.

- **Supervisors** provide guidance and ensure adherence to the recipe, fostering a smooth workflow.

- **Managers** oversee the entire cooking process, making adjustments as needed to ensure the recipe is followed and the final product meets quality standards.

- **Quality control specialists** conduct taste tests and ensure the final product meets the desired flavor profile and visual appearance, just like ensuring the dish looks and tastes delicious.

- **Supply chain managers** guarantee the availability of fresh ingredients, similar to having all the necessary components for the recipe at hand.

- **Engineering teams** maintain the kitchen equipment and appliances, akin to ensuring the stove, oven, and utensils are in good working order.

- **Human resources** create a comfortable and positive environment for the culinary team to work in, just like a well-equipped kitchen fosters a productive atmosphere.

- **Executives** oversee the entire culinary operation, making strategic decisions about the menu, ingredients, and overall dining experience, similar to a restaurant owner setting the vision and direction for the establishment.

This interconnectedness extends beyond the walls of the manufacturing facility. Farmers play a crucial role by providing high-quality raw materials, while transportation and logistics companies ensure timely delivery of these ingredients. Retailers play a vital role in getting the final product onto store shelves, making it accessible to consumers. Each entity within this ecosystem contributes a vital ingredient, and their collaboration ensures a smooth flow from farm to table.

Challenges and Opportunities in the Food Manufacturing Ecosystem

The food manufacturing industry is not without its challenges. Here are some key concerns faced by companies and their workforce:

- **Skilled Labor Gap:** The industry is facing a shortage of skilled workers. Attracting and retaining qualified individuals is crucial for maintaining efficient production.

- **Safety Concerns:** Ensuring a safe work environment for all employees is paramount. Implementing robust safety protocols and fostering a safety culture are essential priorities.

- **Quality Control and Food Safety:** Maintaining strict adherence to regulations and rigorous quality control measures are crucial for preventing foodborne illnesses and ensuring consumer trust.

- **Supply Chain Disruptions:** Unforeseen events like natural disasters or political unrest can disrupt supply chains, leading to shortages and price fluctuations of raw materials.

- **Rising Production Costs:** Optimizing processes and minimizing waste are crucial to keeping production costs under control.

- **Meeting Consumer Demands:** Consumer preferences are constantly evolving. Companies need to adapt to meet these demands, including health-conscious choices and sustainability concerns.

- **Technology Integration:** Embracing automation, robotics, and data analytics can improve efficiency, optimize processes, and provide valuable insights for decision-making.

Challenges:

- **Compliance with stricter food safety regulations:** As food safety becomes a top priority, companies need to constantly adapt their processes to meet evolving regulations.

- **Skilled labor shortage:** Attracting and retaining a skilled workforce with the technical knowledge and experience to operate complex machinery is crucial.

Opportunities:

- **Personalization of food products based on consumer needs:** Consumers are increasingly demanding food options tailored to specific dietary needs, preferences, and allergies.

- **Embracing sustainable practices:** Implementing eco-friendly practices throughout the supply chain can attract environmentally conscious consumers and reduce the industry's environmental impact.

However, these challenges also present opportunities for growth and innovation. The food manufacturing ecosystem is a dynamic and ever-evolving landscape. By fostering a culture of collaboration, continuous learning, and innovation, all the players involved can thrive in the face of challenges. With a dedicated workforce, advanced technology, and a commitment to safety and quality, food manufacturers can continue to deliver diverse and delicious food products that nourish communities worldwide.

Delving Deeper: Specific Roles and Departmental Interactions

The smooth operation of a food manufacturing company hinges on seamless collaboration between various departments. Here's a closer look at some key departments and how they interact to ensure efficient production:

- **Production Planning and Scheduling:**
  - Responsibilities: Analyze customer demand forecasts, translate them into production plans, schedule production runs for specific products.
  - Interactions: Collaborate with **Supply Chain Managers** to ensure the availability of raw materials on time and with **Production Managers** to allocate resources effectively. Imagine a busy restaurant kitchen. The production planning team is like the head chef, assigning tasks to different stations (cooking, baking, etc.) based on the menu and ensuring ingredients are available for each dish.

- **Research and Development (R&D):**
  - Responsibilities: Develop new products, improve existing recipes, explore new technologies and ingredients.
  - Interactions: Collaborate with **Marketing Teams** to understand consumer preferences and with **Quality Control Specialists** to ensure new products meet safety regulations. Think of the R&D team as the culinary innovators, constantly experimenting with new flavor combinations and techniques to create exciting dishes for the menu.

- **Marketing and Sales:**
  - Responsibilities: Develop marketing strategies to promote products, build brand awareness, and reach target markets. Secure distribution channels and negotiate pricing with retailers.

- Interactions: Collaborate with **Finance and Accounting** to determine pricing strategies and with **Production Planning and Scheduling** to ensure sufficient product availability to meet marketing goals. Marketing and sales are like the restaurant's waitstaff and promotional team, enticing customers with the menu's offerings and ensuring a smooth dining experience.

- **Finance and Accounting:**
    - Responsibilities: Manage the financial health of the company. Track costs, revenues, and profitability, ensuring efficient resource allocation. Handle budgeting, payroll, and financial reporting.
    - Interactions: Collaborate with **Production Planning and Scheduling** to understand production costs and with **Purchasing** to manage raw material expenses. Finance and accounting act as the restaurant's bookkeeper, keeping track of expenses, ensuring smooth financial operations, and providing insights for informed decision-making.

This is just a glimpse into the intricate web of interactions between various departments. Effective communication and collaboration are essential for a food manufacturing company's success. By working together, these departments can ensure efficient production, high-quality products, and a satisfied customer base.

Having explored the general landscape of the food manufacturing ecosystem, let's delve deeper into some specific roles and how different departments interact to ensure smooth operations.

- **Production Planning and Scheduling:** This team plays a pivotal role in orchestrating the production flow. They analyze customer demand forecasts, translate them into production plans, and schedule production runs for specific products. They work closely with supply chain managers to ensure the availability of raw materials and with production managers to allocate resources effectively.

Imagine a busy restaurant kitchen. The production planning team is like the head chef, assigning tasks to different stations (cooking, baking, etc.) based on the menu and ensuring ingredients are available for each dish.

- **Research and Development (R&D):** Innovation is key to staying ahead in the competitive food manufacturing industry. R&D teams develop new products, improve existing recipes, and explore new technologies and ingredients. They work closely with marketing teams to understand consumer preferences and with quality control specialists to ensure new products meet safety regulations.

Think of the R&D team as the culinary innovators, constantly experimenting with new flavor combinations and techniques to create exciting dishes for the menu.

- **Marketing and Sales:** This department connects the food manufacturer with consumers. They develop marketing strategies to promote products, build brand awareness, and reach target markets. They also work with sales teams to secure distribution channels and negotiate pricing with retailers.

Marketing and sales are like the restaurant's waitstaff and promotional team, enticing customers with the menu's offerings and ensuring a smooth dining experience.

- **Finance and Accounting:** This department manages the financial health of the company. They track costs, revenues, and profitability, ensuring efficient resource allocation. They also handle budgeting, payroll, and financial reporting.

Finance and accounting act as the restaurant's bookkeeper, keeping track of expenses, ensuring smooth financial operations, and providing insights for informed decision-making.

Interdepartmental Collaboration: The Key to Success

Effective communication and collaboration between these various departments are essential for a food manufacturing company's success. Here are some examples:

- **Production and Quality Control:** Production teams rely on quality control to provide feedback on product consistency and adherence to specifications. This ensures timely adjustments are made to maintain quality standards.

- **Engineering and Maintenance:** Regular communication between these teams is crucial for preventive maintenance and ensuring equipment functionality. This minimizes downtime and production delays.

- **Supply Chain and Production Planning:** Close collaboration ensures raw materials arrive on time and production plans can be adjusted based on any potential supply chain disruptions.

By fostering open communication and collaboration across departments, food manufacturers can create a more efficient, responsive, and innovative ecosystem.

The Future of Food Manufacturing: Embracing Change

The food manufacturing industry is constantly evolving, driven by technological advancements, changing consumer preferences, and global economic trends. Here's a glimpse into some key trends shaping the future:

- **Automation and Robotics:** Integrating automation and robotics into production lines can enhance efficiency, reduce human error, and improve product consistency. However, it's crucial to develop strategies for retraining and upskilling the workforce to adapt to these changes.

- **Data Analytics and Artificial Intelligence (AI):** Utilizing data analytics can provide valuable insights for optimizing processes, predicting maintenance needs, and identifying areas for cost reduction. AI can further enhance decision-making by analyzing vast datasets and recommending optimal production strategies.

- **Sustainability:** Consumers are increasingly concerned about the environmental impact of food production. Companies are focusing on sustainable practices like reducing waste, implementing energy-saving measures, and sourcing ingredients from responsible suppliers.

The food manufacturing ecosystem is a complex yet fascinating web of interconnected roles, each playing a vital role in bringing safe, high-quality food to consumers. By understanding these roles, fostering collaboration, and embracing change, food manufacturers can ensure a sustainable and thriving future for this essential industry.

Empowering the Frontline: A Closer Look

Having explored the broader ecosystem, let's zoom in on the frontline workers, the backbone of food manufacturing. This section will delve deeper into their specific roles, challenges, and opportunities for growth.

A Day in the Life of a Frontline Worker

The daily experiences of frontline workers vary depending on their specific roles. Here are some examples:

- **Machine Operator:** Imagine John, a seasoned machine operator responsible for operating a complex mixing machine. John carefully measures ingredients according to established recipes, ensuring precise proportions for consistent product quality. He monitors the machine's performance, making adjustments as needed to maintain optimal operating parameters. John is also responsible for conducting routine cleaning and sanitation procedures to ensure food safety.

- **Line Worker:** Meet Sarah, a line worker tasked with assembling packaging materials and filling containers with finished products. She meticulously inspects each product for defects or inconsistencies, ensuring only high-quality items reach consumers. Sarah works efficiently within the production line, maintaining a steady flow and adhering to established production targets.

- **Sanitation Technician:** David plays a critical role in maintaining a clean and hygienic environment. He performs regular cleaning and disinfection procedures throughout the production floor, following strict sanitation protocols. David ensures proper disposal of waste materials and sanitizes equipment to prevent the spread of contaminants.

These are just a few examples, and the specific tasks and responsibilities will vary depending on the product being manufactured.

Challenges Faced by Frontline Workers

Despite their vital role, frontline workers often face unique challenges:

- **Repetitive Tasks:** Production line work can be physically demanding and involve repetitive tasks, which can lead to fatigue and potential injuries.

- **Fast-Paced Environment:** Meeting production quotas can create a high-pressure environment, requiring workers to maintain focus and efficiency under tight deadlines.

- **Limited Growth Opportunities:** Frontline workers may perceive limited opportunities for career advancement within the manufacturing industry.

Empowering Frontline Workers for Success

Food manufacturers can implement strategies to empower their frontline workforce and foster a sense of value and ownership:

- **Cross-training:** Providing opportunities for cross-training allows frontline workers to learn new skills and broaden their knowledge base. This can increase their versatility and job satisfaction.

- **Empowerment and Recognition:** Encouraging frontline workers to contribute ideas for process improvement and recognizing their achievements can boost morale and create a sense of ownership.

- **Investment in Training:** Investing in training programs equips frontline workers with the skills and knowledge to perform their jobs effectively and safely. This can include safety training, equipment operation training, and quality control procedures.

- **Clear Communication:** Maintaining open communication channels between frontline workers, supervisors, and management fosters trust and allows for timely resolution of concerns.

The Value Proposition of a Frontline Worker

While the tasks may seem routine, frontline workers play a critical role in the food manufacturing ecosystem. Here's how their contributions translate to value for the company:

- **Quality Assurance:** Their vigilance in adhering to quality control procedures ensures safe and consistent products reach consumers.

- **Efficiency and Productivity:** Their dedication to maintaining production flow keeps the manufacturing process running smoothly and efficiently.

- **Problem-solving:** Frontline workers are often the first to identify potential issues on the production line. Their ability to troubleshoot and report problems helps ensure timely resolution.

- **Innovation:** Valuable insights and suggestions for process improvement can come from frontline workers who have a deep understanding of the daily operations.

The Future of Frontline Workers:

- Increased automation will likely change the landscape of frontline worker roles. While some repetitive tasks might be automated, frontline workers with strong critical thinking, problem-solving, and adaptability skills will be even more valuable.

- Upskilling and continuous learning will be essential for frontline workers to stay relevant in the face of automation. Companies can invest in training programs that equip workers with the skills necessary to operate alongside and manage increasingly sophisticated technology.

Frontline workers are the lifeblood of food manufacturing. By empowering them with the necessary skills, knowledge, and recognition, companies can cultivate a more engaged, productive, and innovative workforce. This, in turn, translates to higher quality products, enhanced efficiency, and a more sustainable food manufacturing ecosystem.

Conclusion: A Symphony of Collaboration

The food manufacturing ecosystem is a complex network of interconnected roles, each playing a vital part in bringing safe, high-quality food to our tables. From the meticulous work of frontline workers to the strategic decisions of executives, every individual contributes a unique note to the symphony of food production.

This chapter has explored the diverse roles within the ecosystem, highlighting the importance of collaboration between departments. We've also delved deeper into the challenges and opportunities faced by frontline workers, the backbone of the industry. By fostering a culture of empowerment, skill development, and recognition, companies can cultivate a more engaged and productive workforce.

As we move forward in this book, we'll explore strategies for addressing the key challenges faced by the food manufacturing industry, such as ensuring a skilled workforce, maintaining the highest levels of safety and quality, and adapting to evolving consumer demands. We'll also delve into the exciting possibilities presented by technological advancements and the growing focus on sustainability.

The future of food manufacturing is bright, and by embracing collaboration, innovation, and a commitment to its workforce, this essential industry can continue to nourish communities worldwide.

CHAPTER 2

Cultivating a Thriving Workforce: Building Skills for Success

The success of any food manufacturing company hinges on its workforce. We explored the diverse roles within the ecosystem. Now, we delve deeper into strategies for building a skilled, engaged, and future-proof workforce equipped to navigate the ever-evolving landscape of food manufacturing.

The Skills Gap Challenge

The food manufacturing industry faces a significant challenge: the skills gap. As experienced workers retire, there's a shortage of qualified individuals to fill their roles. This can lead to production slowdowns, reduced efficiency, and difficulty in adapting to new technologies.

Strategies for Bridging the Gap

Here are some strategies food manufacturers can implement to bridge the skills gap and build a strong workforce:

- **Invest in Training and Development:** Providing comprehensive training programs equips employees with the skills and knowledge to perform their jobs effectively. This can include technical training related to operating specific equipment, hygiene and sanitation protocols, and quality control procedures. Additionally, offering soft skills training in areas like communication, teamwork, and problem-solving can enhance overall performance.

- o In addition to the core training mentioned previously, consider offering targeted programs on:
    - **Safety protocols training:** This could encompass areas like sanitation procedures, hazard identification and prevention, and proper use of personal protective equipment (PPE).
    - **HACCP (Hazard Analysis and Critical Control Points) certification training:** HACCP is a systematic approach to ensuring food safety throughout the entire food chain. Earning a HACCP certification demonstrates a commitment to food safety and can qualify workers for specific roles within the industry.
    - **Soft skills development programs in communication, teamwork, and problem-solving:** These programs can equip employees with the interpersonal skills necessary to collaborate effectively, navigate challenges, and communicate clearly across all levels of the organization.

- **Develop Apprenticeship Programs:** Apprenticeship programs offer a valuable pathway for individuals to gain hands-on experience while earning a living. These programs can be tailored to specific roles within the food manufacturing industry, creating a pipeline of skilled workers for the future.
    - o Apprenticeship programs not only benefit companies by creating a pipeline of pre-trained workers, but they also offer valuable advantages for apprentices. These programs typically combine classroom instruction with on-the-job training under

the guidance of experienced professionals. Apprentices earn wages while gaining practical experience and industry-recognized qualifications, positioning them for successful careers in food manufacturing.

- **Promote from Within:** Identifying and nurturing talent within the existing workforce can be a cost-effective strategy. Providing opportunities for advancement motivates employees, fosters loyalty, and allows them to leverage their institutional knowledge for improved performance.
    - To incentivize internal talent development, create clear career paths that outline the skills and experience required for various positions within the company. Regularly assess employee performance through evaluations and identify high-potential individuals who demonstrate leadership qualities.
    - Invest in mentorship programs that pair these high-potential employees with experienced mentors who can guide their professional development and equip them with the necessary skills to take on larger roles.

- **Partner with Educational Institutions:** Collaboration with local vocational schools and community colleges can provide a steady stream of qualified candidates. Manufacturers can work with educators to develop curriculum aligned with industry needs and offer internship opportunities for students.
    - Collaboration with educational institutions can be mutually beneficial. Food manufacturers can work with vocational schools, community colleges, or universities to:
        - **Co-develop curriculum:** By collaborating with educators, companies can ensure the curriculum aligns with the specific skills and knowledge required for roles within the industry.

- **Offer guest lectures:** Industry professionals can visit schools to share their expertise and provide students with insights into the realities of working in food manufacturing.
- **Develop internship opportunities:** Internship programs offer valuable work experience for students and allow companies to assess potential candidates before hiring full-time.

- **Highlight Career Opportunities:** The food manufacturing industry offers a diverse range of career paths with the potential for growth and advancement. Promoting career opportunities and showcasing the positive aspects of working in the industry can attract new talent.
  - Showcase the diverse range of career paths available within food manufacturing through engaging videos or social media posts that highlight the various roles involved in bringing food products from farm to table.
  - Develop a careers page on the company website that clearly outlines growth opportunities, salary ranges, and the benefits of working in the food manufacturing industry.

The Importance of Continuous Learning

The food manufacturing industry is constantly evolving. New technologies are being developed, consumer preferences are changing, and regulations are being updated. To remain competitive, it's crucial for employees to embrace continuous learning and skill development.

The Looming Skills Gap: A Threat to Industry Stability

The food manufacturing industry faces a significant hurdle: the widening skills gap. As experienced workers retire, a crucial knowledge transfer gap emerges. The challenge lies in finding qualified individuals to fill these roles, potentially leading to:

- **Production Slowdowns:** A shortage of skilled workers can lead to bottlenecks in production lines, impacting output and delivery timelines.

- **Reduced Efficiency:** Inexperienced workers may require more supervision and support, leading to a decline in overall operational efficiency.

- **Difficulty Adapting to New Technologies:** The rapid adoption of automation, robotics, and data analytics requires a workforce adaptable to integrating these technologies into existing workflows.

These challenges can have a ripple effect, impacting not only the efficiency of individual companies but also the overall stability of the food manufacturing industry.

Strategies for Lifelong Learning:

Here's how food manufacturers can foster a culture of lifelong learning and empower their workforce to stay ahead of the curve:

- **Tuition Reimbursement Programs:** Offering financial assistance for employees pursuing further education demonstrates a company's commitment to workforce development and empowers employees to take ownership of their career growth. This can be extended to cover certifications, relevant industry courses, or even college degrees in areas aligned with the company's needs.
    o Tuition reimbursement programs demonstrate a company's commitment to employee development. These programs typically have eligibility requirements and limitations on the

types of degrees or certifications covered. Be sure to clearly outline these details to employees.

- **Invest in Online Learning Resources:** Online learning platforms provide a convenient and accessible way for employees to acquire new skills and knowledge. Companies can subscribe to industry-specific online learning platforms or develop their own internal training modules focusing on emerging technologies, best practices, and regulatory updates.
    - There are numerous industry-specific online learning platforms that offer a variety of courses and certifications relevant to food manufacturing. Examples include The Food Processing Institute, The American Society for Quality (ASQ), and Skillsoft.

- **Encourage Knowledge Sharing:** Creating a culture where employees feel comfortable sharing their expertise with colleagues fosters a collaborative and learning-oriented environment. This can be facilitated through.
    - Foster a culture of knowledge sharing by creating opportunities for employees to learn from each other. Here are a few examples:
        - **Brown bag lunch sessions:** Encourage employees to present on a chosen topic related to their area of expertise during lunchtime sessions.
        - **Internal knowledge-sharing platforms:** Develop an online platform where employees can contribute articles, best practices, or tutorials related to their work. This allows for continuous knowledge sharing and learning within the organization.

- **Mentorship Programs:** Pair experienced employees with newer hires to share knowledge and provide guidance.

- **Knowledge-Sharing Sessions:** Organize regular sessions where employees can present their expertise on specific topics or areas of specialization.

- **Internal Training Initiatives:** Empower employees to develop and deliver internal training sessions on topics they are passionate about or have recently learned.

Building a Culture of Recognition and Engagement

A skilled workforce is only half the battle. To truly thrive, companies need a culture that fosters engagement, motivation, and a sense of belonging. Here's how to achieve this:

- **Performance Recognition:** Recognizing and rewarding employee achievements publicly fosters a sense of accomplishment and motivates employees to strive for excellence. This can take the form of:
    - **Public Recognition Programs:** Acknowledge outstanding contributions during company meetings, newsletters, or internal communication platforms.
    - **Performance Bonuses:** Tie bonuses to achieving specific performance goals or exceeding expectations.
    - **Opportunities for Professional Development:** Offer opportunities for high-performing employees to attend industry conferences, workshops, or leadership training programs.

    Public recognition programs are a great way to motivate employees and acknowledge their achievements. In addition to the examples mentioned previously, consider featuring employee spotlights in company newsletters, highlighting their contributions and accomplishments. Another way to recognize high performers is by assigning them challenging and high-profile projects that allow them to showcase their skills and take ownership of their work.

- **Empowerment and Ownership:** Giving employees ownership over their tasks and encouraging them to contribute ideas for process improvement fosters engagement and a sense of value. This can be achieved by:
    o **Soliciting Feedback:** Regularly solicit employee feedback on production processes, safety procedures, and overall work environment. This demonstrates that their input is valued and can lead to positive changes.
    o **Empowering Decision-Making:** Empower frontline workers to make decisions within their scope of responsibility. This fosters a sense of ownership and accountability.
    o **Celebrating Innovation:** Recognize and reward employees who come up with innovative solutions to improve efficiency, product quality, or safety protocols.

Regularly solicit feedback from employees to demonstrate that their input is valued. Conduct anonymous employee satisfaction surveys to gauge employee morale and identify areas for improvement. Hold regular town hall meetings where employees can openly discuss concerns and suggestions with management.

- **Work-life Balance:** Offering flexible work arrangements, competitive benefits packages, and opportunities for work-life balance promotes employee well-being and reduces turnover. This can include:
    o **Flexible Scheduling:** Consider options like flex hours, compressed workweeks, or telecommuting opportunities to accommodate various employee needs.

- **Competitive Benefits Packages:** Offer health insurance, paid time off, parental leave, and other benefits that demonstrate the company's commitment to employee well-being.
- **Employee Wellness Programs:** Implement initiatives that promote employee well-being, such as on-site fitness centers, healthy food options in cafeterias, or stress management workshops.
- **Open Communication:** Maintaining open lines of communication between employees and management allows for timely resolution of concerns and fosters trust within the organization. This can be achieved through regular employee meetings, anonymous feedback surveys, and open-door policies that encourage employees to voice their concerns or suggestions.

Offering flexible work arrangements, such as compressed workweeks or telecommuting opportunities for eligible positions, can help employees achieve a better work-life balance. Consider providing on-site childcare options or partnering with local childcare providers to ease the burden on working parents.

Building a thriving workforce in food manufacturing requires a multi-faceted approach. By investing in training and development, promoting lifelong learning, and fostering a culture of recognition and engagement, companies can bridge the skills gap, cultivate a more engaged workforce, and ensure long-term success in the ever-evolving landscape of the food manufacturing industry.

Bridging the Gap: Strategies for Building a Strong Workforce

The good news is that there are proactive strategies food manufacturers can implement to bridge the skills gap and build a robust talent pipeline:

1. Investing in Training and Development:

This isn't a one-time fix. A continuous learning environment is key. Here's a breakdown:

- **Technical Training:** This equips employees with the skills and knowledge needed to perform their specific roles effectively. Examples include operating machinery, following sanitation protocols, and conducting quality control checks.
    - **On-the-Job Training:** Seasoned employees can mentor and train new hires, providing valuable hands-on experience and fostering a culture of knowledge sharing.
    - **Specialized Training Programs:** Develop comprehensive training programs tailored to specific roles or equipment. Partner with industry experts or equipment manufacturers to create customized training modules.
- **Soft Skills Training:** These skills are essential for effective teamwork, communication, and problem-solving in any work environment. Examples include:
    - **Communication Skills:** Effective communication across all levels – frontline workers to supervisors to management – is crucial for smooth operations. Training programs can focus on clear and concise communication, active listening, and conflict resolution.
    - **Teamwork Skills:** Food manufacturing is a collaborative effort. Teamwork training can help employees develop skills in collaboration, building trust within teams, and achieving shared goals.
    - **Problem-Solving Skills:** Unexpected issues can arise on the production floor. Training employees in critical thinking,

creative problem-solving techniques, and effective decision-making can empower them to address challenges efficiently.

2. Developing Apprenticeship Programs:

These programs offer a valuable pathway for individuals to gain valuable hands-on experience while earning a living:

- **Structured Learning:** Apprenticeship programs combine classroom instruction with on-the-job training under the guidance of experienced workers. This allows apprentices to develop a strong foundation in theoretical knowledge and practical skills simultaneously.

- **Career Path Development:** Design apprenticeship programs with clear career progression pathways. Upon completion, apprentices can transition smoothly into full-time skilled positions within the company.

- **Collaboration with Educational Institutions:** Partner with vocational schools, community colleges, or universities to develop curriculum aligned with industry needs. These institutions can provide the theoretical foundation, while apprenticeship programs at food manufacturing companies offer practical application.

3. Promoting from Within:

Looking within your existing workforce can be a cost-effective strategy to fill open positions:

- **Identifying Talent:** Implement performance review systems that identify high-performing employees with leadership potential.

- **Mentorship Programs:** Pair these high-potential employees with experienced mentors who can guide their professional development and equip them with the necessary skills to take on larger roles.

- **Succession Planning:** Develop a long-term succession plan that identifies future leadership positions and creates a pipeline of qualified employees prepared to step into those roles. This demonstrates a commitment to employee development and loyalty.

4. Partnering with Educational Institutions:

Building a strong relationship with educational institutions can create a steady stream of qualified candidates:

- **Curriculum Development:** Collaborate with educators to develop curriculum that aligns with the specific skills and knowledge required for roles within the food manufacturing industry.

- **Internship Opportunities:** Provide internship opportunities for students enrolled in relevant programs. Internships offer valuable work experience and allow companies to assess potential candidates before hiring full-time.

- **Career Fairs:** Participating in career fairs at vocational schools, community colleges, and universities allows companies to showcase their organization and attract potential candidates.

5. Highlighting Career Opportunities:

The food manufacturing industry offers a diverse range of career paths with the potential for growth and advancement, but it may not always be readily apparent to potential candidates. Here's how to showcase the industry's appeal:

- **Marketing Efforts:** Develop marketing materials that showcase the various career paths available within food manufacturing. Highlight opportunities for growth, competitive salaries and benefits packages, and the positive impact the industry has on society by providing safe and nutritious food.

- **Social Media Engagement:** Utilize social media platforms to showcase the diverse roles within your company and the positive aspects of working in food manufacturing. Share employee testimonials, behind-the-scenes glimpses of production processes, and career development opportunities.

- **Community Outreach:** Engage with local schools and community organizations to educate students and young adults about the opportunities within the food manufacturing industry. Organize career days or industry tours to spark interest and showcase the dynamic nature of the field.

Beyond Skills: Cultivating a Learning Culture

The food manufacturing industry is constantly evolving. New technologies are emerging, consumer preferences are shifting rapidly, and regulations are being updated. To remain competitive, it's crucial for employees to embrace a culture of continuous learning and skill development.

Cultivating a Thriving Workforce: Empowering Frontline Workers

Highlighting the interconnectedness of each function. Then we focused on building a skilled and engaged workforce through various strategies, including training and development, apprenticeship programs, and fostering a culture of recognition. Now, we delve deeper into the concept of empowering frontline workers – the backbone of the food manufacturing industry.

The Power of Empowerment: A Catalyst for Improved Performance

Empowering frontline workers is not simply a feel-good notion; it's a strategic approach that yields significant benefits for both employees and the company. Here's why:

- **Increased Ownership and Accountability:** When frontline workers feel empowered to make decisions within their scope of responsibility, they take greater ownership of their work and become more accountable for the outcomes. This fosters a sense of pride and accomplishment, leading to higher levels of motivation and engagement.

- **Improved Problem-Solving and Innovation:** Frontline workers are often the first to identify potential issues or inefficiencies on the production floor. Empowering them to share their insights and participate in problem-solving can lead to innovative solutions and continuous improvement.

- **Enhanced Job Satisfaction and Reduced Turnover:** Feeling valued, trusted, and having the opportunity to contribute beyond their basic tasks leads to increased job satisfaction. This, in turn, reduces employee turnover, a significant cost for any organization.

- **Improved Efficiency and Productivity:** Empowering frontline workers to make informed decisions based on real-time production data allows for quicker adjustments and streamlined processes, ultimately enhancing overall efficiency and productivity.

Strategies for Empowering Your Frontline Workforce:

Moving beyond simply providing training, here's how food manufacturers can create an environment that empowers frontline workers:

1. Fostering a Culture of Open Communication:

- **Two-Way Communication Channels:** Establish clear and open communication channels that allow frontline workers to voice their concerns, suggestions, and ideas. This can be achieved through regular team meetings, suggestion boxes, or anonymous feedback surveys.

- **Active Listening:** Management must actively listen to feedback from frontline workers and demonstrate that their input is valued. Address concerns promptly and transparently, and provide explanations when suggestions are not implemented.

- **Transparency and Information Sharing:** Keep frontline workers informed about company goals, performance metrics, and any changes that may impact their work. This transparency fosters trust and a sense of being part of a larger team.

2. Encouraging Knowledge Sharing and Collaboration:

- **Mentorship Programs:** Pair experienced frontline workers with newer hires to share knowledge, best practices, and provide guidance. This fosters a collaborative learning environment and empowers experienced workers to take on leadership roles.

- **Cross-Training Opportunities:** Providing opportunities for cross-training allows frontline workers to gain a broader understanding of different aspects of the production process. This versatility can be invaluable in addressing staffing shortages or unforeseen production challenges.

- **Teamwork Recognition:** Recognize and reward outstanding teamwork that exemplifies collaboration and problem-solving skills.

This can incentivize collaborative efforts and highlight the value of working together.

3. Providing Opportunities for Decision-Making:

- **Task Delegation:** Delegate specific tasks and decision-making authority to frontline workers within their area of expertise. This empowers them to take ownership of their work and make informed decisions based on their knowledge and experience.

- **Problem-Solving Teams:** Create cross-functional teams consisting of frontline workers and other departments to address specific challenges or opportunities for improvement. This allows frontline workers to contribute their unique perspective and participate in finding solutions.

- **Pilot Programs and Experimentation:** Encourage frontline workers to propose and pilot new ideas for improving processes or product quality. This demonstrates trust in their abilities and fosters a culture of innovation.

4. Investing in Continuous Learning and Development:

- **Skills Development Programs:** While technical skills training is essential, consider offering soft skills development programs to enhance communication, teamwork, and problem-solving abilities. These skills empower frontline workers to interact effectively with colleagues, identify and solve problems collaboratively, and lead by example.

- **Microlearning Opportunities:** Provide bite-sized learning modules or training sessions that can be easily integrated into busy work schedules. Microlearning allows for continuous skill development without disrupting production workflows.

- **Leadership Development for Frontline Workers:** Invest in leadership development programs to empower frontline workers who demonstrate potential to take on supervisory or leadership roles within the organization. This demonstrates a commitment to internal growth and provides clear career progression opportunities.

5. Recognition and Appreciation:

- **Public Recognition Programs:** Publicly acknowledge and reward outstanding contributions from frontline workers. This can be done during team meetings, company newsletters, or through an employee-of-the-month program. Public recognition fosters a sense of accomplishment and motivates others to strive for excellence.

- **Performance-Based Incentives:** Consider implementing performance-based incentive programs that reward frontline workers for exceeding production goals, achieving quality benchmarks, or identifying and resolving critical issues. This ties recognition directly to performance and motivates continuous improvement.

- **Celebrating Milestones:** Acknowledge and celebrate individual and team milestones, such as reaching production targets, achieving safety goals, or completing a successful training program. Celebrating these milestones reinforces positive behaviors and strengthens team spirit.

- **Empowering Through Technology:** Technology can be a powerful tool for empowering frontline workers. Here are some ways to leverage technology:

- **Real-time Data Access:** Providing frontline workers with access to real-time production data allows them to make informed decisions based on current conditions. This can involve equipping them with mobile devices or tablets that display key performance indicators (KPIs), allowing them to monitor progress, identify potential issues, and adjust their work accordingly.

- **Digital Collaboration Tools:** Utilizing digital collaboration platforms fosters communication and knowledge sharing between frontline workers, supervisors, and other departments. These platforms can be used for sharing best practices, documenting procedures, and collaborating on problem-solving efforts.

- **Performance Management Apps:** Performance management applications can streamline feedback mechanisms, allowing for regular check-ins between frontline workers and supervisors. These apps can also facilitate goal setting, track progress towards objectives, and provide opportunities for self-directed learning.

- **Addressing Challenges and Overcoming Obstacles:** Empowering frontline workers is not without its challenges:

- **Resistance to Change:** Some managers may be hesitant to relinquish control or share decision-making authority. Addressing these concerns through clear communication and demonstrating the benefits of empowerment can help overcome resistance.

- **Lack of Training and Support:** Frontline workers may require additional training or support to take on new responsibilities and make informed decisions. Providing comprehensive training programs and ongoing mentorship is crucial for success.

- **Performance Measurement:** Measuring the impact of empowerment on performance can be challenging. However, focusing on metrics like productivity, quality improvement, employee satisfaction, and innovation can provide valuable insights.

- **Building a Culture of Continuous Improvement:** Empowerment is not a one-time event; it's an ongoing process. Here's how to ensure continuous improvement:

- **Regular Feedback and Evaluation:** Regularly solicit feedback from frontline workers on the effectiveness of empowerment initiatives. Use this feedback to identify areas for improvement and adapt the approach as needed.

- **Celebrating Success Stories:** Highlight successful examples of empowered frontline workers making positive contributions. Sharing these stories reinforces the value of empowerment and inspires others to take ownership and initiative.

- **Leadership Commitment:** Empowerment requires a genuine commitment from leadership. Leaders must demonstrate a willingness to trust frontline workers, listen to their ideas, and provide the necessary support for them to succeed.

Empowering frontline workers is not simply a feel-good practice; it's a strategic investment in the future of your food manufacturing operation. By fostering a culture of open communication, encouraging knowledge sharing, providing opportunities for decision-making, and investing in continuous learning and development, food manufacturers can empower their frontline workforce to become active participants in achieving organizational goals. This empowered workforce will be more engaged, innovative, and ultimately contribute to a thriving and successful food manufacturing company.

CHAPTER 3

Ensuring the Highest Standards of Safety and Quality: A Top Priority

The foundation of a successful food manufacturing operation rests on two paramount pillars: safety and quality. We explored the ecosystem of roles within the industry, and We focused on building a skilled and engaged workforce. Now, we delve into the critical strategies for ensuring the highest standards of safety and quality throughout the entire food production process.

Safety First: A Commitment to Worker Wellbeing

Food manufacturing environments can present inherent risks. Machinery operation, working with sharp tools, and potential exposure to chemicals necessitate a rigorous commitment to safety procedures. Here's how to prioritize worker wellbeing:

- **Comprehensive Safety Training:** All employees, regardless of role, must undergo comprehensive safety training. This training should cover:
  - **Hazard Identification and Risk Assessment:** Equipping employees to identify potential hazards within their work environment and understand the associated risks.

- **Safe Work Practices:** Training on proper safety procedures for operating machinery, handling equipment, and using personal protective equipment (PPE).
- **Emergency Response Protocols:** Employees should be trained on how to respond to emergencies like fires, spills, or medical incidents.
- **Regular Refresher Courses:** Conducting regular refresher courses ensures that safety protocols remain top-of-mind and employees are updated on any changes.
- **Hazard Communication:** Training employees on identifying hazardous materials, understanding Safety Data Sheets (SDS), and proper handling procedures.
- **Ergonomics:** Equipping employees with proper lifting techniques and workstation setup to prevent musculoskeletal disorders.
- **Lockout/Tagout Procedures:** Training on safely isolating and de-energizing machinery before performing maintenance or repairs.

- **Investing in Safe Equipment:** Investing in well-maintained, up-to-date machinery and equipment minimizes the risk of malfunctions or accidents. Regular equipment inspections and preventive maintenance programs are crucial.
  - Aside from regular inspections and preventive maintenance, consider incorporating:
    - **Guarding and Machine Safety:** Ensuring machinery has proper guards and safety interlocks to prevent accidental contact with moving parts.
    - **Personal Protective Equipment (PPE):** Providing appropriate PPE for various tasks, such as safety glasses, gloves, respirators, and ear protection.

- **Promoting a Culture of Safety:** Building a safety culture goes beyond training. It fosters a shared responsibility for safety within the organization. Here's how:
    - **Visible Management Commitment:** Leadership should visibly demonstrate their commitment to safety by regularly participating in safety inspections, addressing safety concerns promptly, and recognizing safe work practices.
    - **Employee Participation:** Encourage employees to report unsafe conditions or practices without fear of reprisal. Develop employee-led safety committees to create a sense of ownership and accountability.
    - **Positive Reinforcement:** Recognize and reward employees who consistently adhere to safety protocols and take initiative to improve safety standards.
    - **Incentive Programs:** Implement programs that reward employees for adhering to safety protocols, identifying hazards, or suggesting safety improvements.
    - **Safety Committees:** Empower employee-led safety committees to conduct regular inspections, investigate incidents, and recommend improvements.
    - **Near Miss Reporting:** Encourage employees to report near misses without fear of reprisal. This allows for proactive identification and mitigation of potential hazards.

A Multi-layered Approach to Maintaining Quality

Ensuring food quality goes beyond simply delivering a tasty product. It encompasses safety, consistency, and meeting regulatory standards. Here's a breakdown of the strategies employed:

- **Quality Management Systems (QMS):** Implementing a robust QMS provides a framework for monitoring and maintaining quality throughout the entire production process. This can involve:
    - **Hazard Analysis and Critical Control Points (HACCP):** HACCP is a systematic approach to identifying, preventing, and controlling potential food safety hazards at critical control points within the production process.
    - **Good Manufacturing Practices (GMPs):** GMPs are a set of guidelines that ensure consistent quality by establishing procedures for sanitation, production, and equipment maintenance.
    - **Standard Operating Procedures (SOPs):** Developing and adhering to SOPs ensures consistency in every step of the production process, from receiving raw materials to packaging finished products.
    - **SQF (Safe Quality Food):** A globally recognized food safety and quality certification program.
    - **ISO 22000:** A set of international standards for food safety management systems.
- **Rigorous Quality Control Measures:** Throughout the production process, quality control checks are implemented at various stages:
    - **Incoming Ingredient Inspection:** Raw materials are rigorously inspected upon arrival to ensure they meet established quality standards and specifications.

- **In-Process Inspection:** Throughout production, samples are taken and tested at various stages to identify any deviations from quality standards.
- **Finished Product Testing:** Final products undergo rigorous testing to ensure they meet all safety and quality parameters before being released for distribution.
- **In-Process Controls:** Conducting online monitoring of critical control points during production, such as temperature or pressure checks.
- **Finished Product Testing:** Performing sensory evaluation by trained personnel to assess taste, texture, and appearance of finished products.
- **Microbiological Testing:** Testing products for the presence of harmful bacteria or pathogens to ensure food safety.

- **Continuous Improvement:** Maintaining the highest quality standards is an ongoing process. Here's how to ensure continuous improvement:
  - **Data Analysis:** Analyze data collected through quality control measures to identify trends and areas for improvement.
  - **Root Cause Analysis:** Investigate the root causes of any quality issues to prevent their recurrence.
  - **Embracing New Technologies:** Explore and adopt new technologies that enhance quality control, such as automated product inspection systems or real-time data monitoring of production processes.
  - **Benchmarking:** Comparing your company's performance metrics with industry leaders to identify areas for improvement.
  - **Customer Feedback Mechanisms:** Actively collecting customer feedback through surveys or focus groups to

understand their preferences and identify areas for product improvement.
  - **Employee Engagement:** Encouraging employees to suggest improvements to quality control processes or product specifications.

Navigating the Regulatory Landscape

The food manufacturing industry operates within a complex framework of regulations. Complying with these regulations is vital for ensuring food safety and consumer trust. Here's how companies navigate this landscape:

- **Maintaining Regulatory Knowledge:** Food manufacturers must stay updated on all relevant local, national, and international food safety regulations. This may involve subscribing to regulatory updates, attending industry conferences, or consulting with food safety specialists.

- **Developing Compliance Programs:** Establish comprehensive compliance programs that ensure adherence to all applicable regulations. This may involve conducting regular audits, documenting procedures, and maintaining detailed records.
  - Standard Operating Procedures (SOPs) for all aspects of food production, from receiving raw materials to shipping finished products.
  - Detailed record-keeping of all processes, inspections, and test results.
  - Regular internal audits to identify and address any gaps in compliance.

- **Collaboration with Regulatory Agencies:** Maintain a positive and collaborative relationship with regulatory agencies. This can be

achieved through open communication, promptly addressing any concerns raised during inspections, and proactively seeking guidance on regulatory changes.
   - Inviting regulatory inspectors for pre-inspection consultations to ensure readiness for official inspections.
   - Scheduling regular meetings with regulatory agencies to discuss upcoming changes in regulations or industry best practices.

- **The Intersection of Safety and Quality: A Shared Goal:** Safety and quality are not isolated concepts in food manufacturing; they are intertwined. By prioritizing safety, companies create a work environment where employees feel comfortable raising concerns about potential quality issues. Conversely, maintaining high-quality standards reduces the risk of accidents or contamination. This holistic approach fosters a culture of excellence throughout the organization.

- **The Cost of Cutting Corners: Why Safety and Quality Matter:** While prioritizing safety and quality may seem like an added expense, the consequences of neglecting these areas can be far more costly:

- **Product Recalls:** A single product recall can have a devastating impact on a company's reputation, financial stability, and consumer trust.

- **Lawsuits:** Foodborne illnesses or product defects can lead to costly lawsuits and settlements.

- **Loss of Consumer Trust:** Consumers expect safe, high-quality food. Failing to meet these expectations can result in a significant decline in sales and brand loyalty. Investing in safety and quality is not just an ethical imperative, it's a sound business decision.

- **The Future of Food Safety and Quality: Embracing Innovation:** The food manufacturing industry is constantly evolving, and so too are the approaches to safety and quality. Here's a glimpse into some of the key trends shaping the future:

- **Automation and Robotics:** Integrating automation and robotics into quality control processes can enhance accuracy, efficiency, and consistency. For example, automated vision systems can inspect products for defects at a much faster rate and with greater precision than human inspectors.

- **Internet of Things (IoT) and Big Data:** Utilizing IoT sensors and real-time data collection allows for continuous monitoring of production processes, storage conditions, and product quality throughout the supply chain. This data can be used to identify potential issues early on and take preventive measures.

- **Blockchain Technology:** Blockchain technology can be leveraged to enhance food traceability, allowing consumers to track the origin of ingredients and ensure the authenticity of products. By embracing these innovations, food manufacturers can further elevate their safety and quality standards, building trust with consumers and ensuring a sustainable future for the industry.

Ensuring the highest standards of safety and quality is at the core of every successful food manufacturing operation. By implementing comprehensive safety training programs, fostering a culture of safety, and adhering to rigorous quality control measures, companies can create a work environment where employees feel valued and empowered to produce safe, high-quality food products. Furthermore, staying abreast of regulations and embracing new technologies can solidify a company's position as a leader within the evolving food manufacturing landscape.

Embracing Innovation: Navigating the Challenges and Opportunities of the Future

The food manufacturing industry, like any other, is constantly evolving. New technologies are emerging, consumer preferences are shifting rapidly, and the global landscape is constantly in flux. To remain competitive and thrive in this dynamic environment, food manufacturers must be adaptable and embrace innovation. This chapter explores the key challenges and opportunities facing the industry, along with innovative solutions that can propel companies towards a successful future.

The Looming Challenges: Navigating a Complex Landscape

Food manufacturers face a multitude of challenges that threaten their stability and growth:

- **The Rising Cost of Raw Materials:** Fluctuations in global commodity prices, climate change impacting crop yields, and increasing competition for resources can lead to unpredictable and often rising costs of raw materials.

- **Shifting Consumer Preferences:** Consumers are increasingly demanding healthy, sustainable, and ethically sourced food products. Meeting these evolving preferences requires constant adaptation and innovation.

- **The Growing Threat of Foodborne Illness:** Food safety remains a paramount concern. Emerging pathogens, complex supply chains, and the need for efficient yet safe food production methods require constant vigilance and innovation.

- **Labor Shortages:** The skills gap discussed in Chapter 2 is a significant challenge. Attracting and retaining a skilled workforce is crucial for continued success.

- **Sustainability Concerns:** Consumers are more environmentally conscious than ever before. The industry needs to find ways to minimize its environmental footprint and adopt sustainable practices throughout the supply chain.

These challenges, while formidable, also present opportunities for innovation and differentiation.

Innovation: A Catalyst for Growth

Innovation plays a critical role in enabling food manufacturers to overcome challenges and seize opportunities. Here are some key areas where innovation is transforming the industry:

- **Product Development:**
    - **Focus on Functional Foods:** Developing food products that offer health benefits beyond basic nutrition, such as prebiotics, probiotics, or fortified foods with added vitamins and minerals.
    - **Plant-Based Alternatives:** The demand for plant-based meat and dairy alternatives is surging. Innovation in plant-based ingredients and product development is crucial to meet this growing consumer demand.
    - **Personalized Nutrition:** The rise of personalized nutrition concepts offers opportunities to develop food products tailored to individual dietary needs and preferences.

- **Advanced Manufacturing Technologies:**
    - **Automation and Robotics:** Integrating automation and robotics into production lines can improve efficiency, consistency, and safety. Automation can handle repetitive tasks, freeing up human workers to focus on higher-level functions.

- o **Additive Manufacturing (3D Printing):** 3D printing has the potential to revolutionize food production, allowing for the creation of customized food products with complex shapes and textures.
- o **Artificial Intelligence (AI) and Machine Learning:** Utilizing AI and machine learning can optimize production processes, predict potential issues, and improve overall efficiency.

- **The Rise of E-commerce and Direct-to-Consumer (D2C) Models:**
  - o **E-commerce platforms** provide new channels for directly reaching consumers and expanding market reach.
  - o **Subscription-based services** delivering curated food products to consumers' doorsteps are gaining traction.

- **Sustainable Practices:**
  - o **Reducing Food Waste:** Developing innovative solutions to minimize food waste throughout the supply chain, from farm to fork.
  - o **Sustainable Packaging:** Transitioning to recyclable, biodegradable, or compostable packaging materials can significantly reduce the industry's environmental footprint.
  - o **Renewable Energy Sources:** Adopting renewable energy sources like solar or wind power can lessen the industry's reliance on fossil fuels and reduce its carbon footprint.

The Road Ahead: Embracing Change and Continuous Learning

The future of food manufacturing belongs to those who embrace change, cultivate a culture of innovation, and continuously invest in learning and development. This requires:

- **Building a Culture of Innovation:** Fostering a company culture that encourages creativity, risk-taking, and collaboration is essential for generating innovative ideas.

- **Investing in Research and Development (R&D):** Dedicating resources to R&D allows companies to stay at the forefront of technological advancements and develop new products and processes.

- **Partnerships and Collaboration:** Collaboration with research institutions, universities, and startups can accelerate innovation and bring new ideas to the table.

- **Embracing a Growth Mindset:** A continuous learning mindset across all levels of the organization is crucial for adapting to change and remaining competitive.

By embracing these strategies, food manufacturers can navigate the challenges and opportunities of the future, ensuring their long-term success and contributing to a more secure, sustainable, and innovative food system.

Case Studies: Innovation in Action

To illustrate the power of innovation, let's explore a few real-world examples:

- **Example 1: Utilizing AI for Predictive Maintenance:** Imagine a food manufacturing company employing AI-powered sensors throughout its production line. These sensors can continuously monitor equipment performance and predict potential failures before they occur. This allows for proactive maintenance, minimizing downtime, reducing waste, and ultimately enhancing overall efficiency.

- **Example 2: Vertical Farming for Urban Food Production:** Vertical farming utilizes controlled environments and innovative techniques to grow crops in vertically stacked layers. This can be a game-changer in urban areas with limited space for traditional agriculture. Vertical farms can produce fresh, high-quality produce year-round, with a smaller environmental footprint compared to conventional farming methods.

- **Example 3: Blockchain Technology for Supply Chain Transparency:** Blockchain technology offers a secure and transparent way to track food products throughout the supply chain. This allows consumers to trace the origin of their food, ensuring authenticity and ethical sourcing practices. For companies, blockchain can streamline logistics, improve traceability, and enhance consumer trust.

These are just a few examples of how innovation is transforming the food manufacturing industry. Companies that stay ahead of the curve and embrace these transformative advancements will be well-positioned to thrive in the years to come.

The future of food manufacturing is bright and brimming with possibilities. However, it also presents a complex landscape with its own set of challenges. By embracing innovation, fostering a culture of continuous learning, and prioritizing safety, quality, and sustainability, food manufacturers can overcome hurdles, contribute to a more secure global food system, and ultimately, nourish a healthier, more conscious generation of consumers.

CHAPTER 4

Leading from the Front: Strategies for Supervisors

Supervisors are the backbone of any successful food manufacturing operation. They act as the crucial bridge between frontline workers and upper management, playing a vital role in ensuring smooth production flow, maintaining high standards of safety and quality, and motivating their teams to achieve organizational goals. This chapter explores the key strategies and qualities that empower supervisors to become effective leaders "from the front."

The Making of a Great Supervisor: More Than Just a manager

Effective supervisors go beyond simply managing tasks and overseeing production. They are leaders who inspire, motivate, and empower their teams. Here's what distinguishes a great supervisor:

- **Strong Communication Skills:** Supervisors need exceptional communication skills—both verbal and written—to convey instructions clearly, provide constructive feedback, and actively listen to their team members' concerns, ideas, and suggestions.
    - Clearly explain new procedures or tasks using step-by-step instructions and demonstrations.

- Actively listen to employee concerns by maintaining eye contact, asking clarifying questions, and summarizing key points.
- Provide constructive feedback using the "feedback sandwich" method: starting with positive reinforcement, then offering specific areas for improvement, and concluding with encouragement.

- **Technical Expertise:** Understanding the intricacies of the production process is crucial. It allows supervisors to effectively train new team members, troubleshoot problems, and answer questions with confidence.
    - Understanding the functionalities and proper operation of relevant equipment.
    - Being able to identify and troubleshoot common production problems.
    - Possessing a working knowledge of food safety regulations and quality control procedures.

- **Decision-Making Skills:** Supervisors have the autonomy to make critical decisions on the production floor. They need to be able to analyze situations, weigh options, and make sound decisions that prioritize safety, quality, and efficiency.

- **Problem-Solving Skills:** Inevitably, problems arise on the production floor. Supervisors need to be adept at identifying the root causes of issues, brainstorming solutions, and implementing effective corrective actions.

- **Building Trust and Rapport:** Effective supervisors foster a positive and trusting relationship with their team members. This involves open communication, empathy, and recognizing individual contributions.

- **Delegation and Empowerment:** Micromanagement stifles initiative and innovation. Great supervisors delegate tasks effectively, empowering their team members to take ownership and make decisions within their scope of responsibility.

- **Coaching and Mentoring Skills:** Supervisors play a crucial role in developing their team members' skills and knowledge. Providing effective coaching and mentorship empowers employees to grow professionally and reach their full potential.

- **Leading by Example:** Effective leaders inspire by example. They demonstrate the behaviors and work ethic they expect from their team members, fostering a culture of professionalism and commitment.

Cultivating a High-Performing Team: Strategies for Success

Supervisors play a critical role in building and nurturing high-performing teams. Here are some key strategies:

1. Setting Clear Goals and Expectations:

- **Alignment with Organizational Goals:** Ensure team goals align with the overall objectives of the organization. This fosters a sense of purpose and connects individual work to the bigger picture.

- **SMART Goals:** Set Specific, Measurable, Achievable, Relevant, and Time-bound (SMART) goals for each team member and the team as a whole. This provides clarity, direction, and a framework for measuring progress.
    - Here's an example of a SMART goal for a team:
        - **Specific:** Reduce production line downtime by 5%.

- **Measurable:** Track downtime through a data collection system.
- **Achievable:** Set a realistic target that is challenging but attainable.
- **Relevant:** Reducing downtime directly improves production efficiency.
- **Time-bound:** Achieve the goal within the next quarter.

- **Open Communication and Collaboration:** Involve team members in the goal-setting process whenever possible. This encourages ownership and buy-in, fostering a collaborative work environment.

2. Providing Ongoing Training and Development:

- **Identify Skills Gaps:** Regularly assess the skills and knowledge gaps within your team. This can be done through performance reviews, individual discussions, or analyzing production data.

- **Tailored Training Programs:** Develop personalized training programs catering to the specific needs of each team member. This could involve on-the-job training, mentorship opportunities, or external training courses.

- **Investing in Continuous Learning:** Encourage a culture of continuous learning within your team. Provide access to industry publications, online learning resources, and opportunities for cross-training.
    - Examples of tailored training programs:
        - Develop a skills matrix to identify individual skill gaps within the team.
        - For employees struggling with machine operation, provide targeted training sessions on specific equipment.

- For employees with leadership potential, offer mentorship opportunities or leadership development courses.

3. Fostering Open Communication and Feedback:

- **Two-Way Communication Channels:** Create an environment where team members feel comfortable expressing their ideas, concerns, and suggestions.

- **Active Listening:** Actively listen to your team members and demonstrate value for their input. Provide regular feedback, both positive and constructive, to help them improve their performance.

- **Open-Door Policy:** Maintain an open-door policy, allowing team members to approach you with questions, concerns, or simply to share ideas. This fosters trust and demonstrates accessibility.
  - Examples of open-door policy:
    - Schedule regular one-on-one meetings with team members to discuss their concerns and progress.
    - Maintain an open-door policy by keeping your office door open and approachable.
    - Encourage employees to communicate any safety hazards or potential issues immediately.

4. Recognizing and Rewarding Achievements:

- **Formal Recognition Programs:** Implement formal recognition programs to acknowledge and reward outstanding performance. This can involve public recognition, performance bonuses, or opportunities for professional development.

- **Informal Recognition:** Provide regular informal recognition for a job well done. A simple "thank you" or acknowledging a team member's efforts can go a long way in boosting morale.

- **Celebrating Milestones:** Celebrate individual and team milestones, such as achieving production targets, exceeding safety goals, or completing a successful training program. This reinforces positive behaviors and strengthens team spirit.
  - Examples of informal recognition:
    - Publicly acknowledge a team member's accomplishment during a team meeting.
    - Provide a handwritten thank-you note expressing appreciation for a job well done.
    - Offer additional responsibilities or challenging tasks to high-performing team members.

5. Promoting Teamwork:

- **Collaborative Problem-Solving:** Encourage team members to collaborate on solving problems and tackling challenges. This fosters a sense of shared responsibility and leverages the diverse strengths of individual team members.

- **Team-Building Activities:** Organize team-building activities that promote collaboration, communication, and trust-building among team members.

- **Shared Goals and Incentives:** Establish shared team goals and tie incentives to achieving those goals collectively. This fosters collaboration and a sense of working together towards a common objective.

Building a Culture of Safety and Quality: A Shared Responsibility

Supervisors are at the forefront of ensuring a safe and quality-driven work environment. Here's how they contribute:

- **Safety Leadership:** Supervisors set the tone for safety on the production floor. This involves leading by example, strictly adhering to safety protocols, and actively identifying and addressing potential hazards.
    - Examples of safety leadership:
        - Always wear required personal protective equipment (PPE) and follow safety protocols.
        - Conduct regular safety inspections and address any identified hazards promptly.
        - Recognize and reward team members who consistently adhere to safety procedures.

- **Safety Training and Enforcement:** Supervisors are responsible for ensuring their team members receive comprehensive safety training and understand all safety procedures. They also play a crucial role in enforcing safety rules and holding team members accountable for following them.
    - Specific examples of safety training:
        - Fire safety training, including extinguisher use and evacuation procedures.
        - Bloodborne pathogen training to prevent the spread of infectious diseases.
        - Machine-specific safety training on proper operation and lockout/tagout procedures.

- **Quality Control:** Supervisors play a vital role in maintaining quality standards. This involves monitoring production processes, inspecting products for defects, and immediately addressing any quality issues that arise.

- **Continuous Improvement:** Supervisors can be valuable assets in identifying areas for improvement within their teams and processes. Encourage them to share their insights and participate in continuous improvement initiatives.

Leveraging Technology for Effective Supervision: Tools and Resources

Technology can be a powerful tool for supervisors, enhancing their effectiveness and efficiency:

- **Production Monitoring Systems:** Real-time data from production monitoring systems allows supervisors to identify potential issues early on, optimize production flow, and make informed decisions.
    - Examples of data monitored through production monitoring systems:
        - Real-time machine performance data to identify potential equipment failures before they occur.
        - Production line speed and output to ensure efficient production flow.
        - Temperature and humidity data in critical areas to maintain optimal storage conditions for ingredients and finished products.
- **Performance Management Software:** Performance management software can streamline the process of setting goals, tracking progress, and providing feedback to team members.
    - Specific functionalities of performance management software:
        - Setting and tracking individual and team performance goals.

- Providing online performance reviews and feedback.
- Documenting employee training records and certifications.

- **Communication and Collaboration Tools:** Digital communication and collaboration tools facilitate seamless communication between supervisors, team members, and other departments, enhancing coordination and information sharing.

The Challenges of Supervision and Overcoming Obstacles

Supervisors face unique challenges in their roles:

- **Balancing Production Demands with Team Needs:** Supervisors often find themselves caught between meeting production quotas and ensuring the well-being of their team members. Effective communication, delegation, and prioritizing tasks are crucial for navigating this balance.
  - Strategies for balancing production demands with team needs:
    - Delegate tasks effectively to empower team members and avoid micromanagement.
    - Prioritize tasks based on importance and urgency to ensure deadlines are met while allowing breaks for employee well-being.
    - Communicate production demands clearly to the team and explain the rationale behind them.

- **Managing Conflict:** Disagreements or conflicts can arise within teams. Supervisors need to be adept at facilitating constructive conversations, mediating conflict resolution, and fostering a positive work environment.
  - Steps for addressing performance issues effectively:
    - Document specific examples of underperformance.

- Schedule a private meeting with the employee to discuss the concerns and potential solutions.
- Develop a corrective action plan with clear expectations and timelines for improvement.
- Provide ongoing coaching and support to help the employee improve their performance.

- **Dealing with Difficult Personalities:** Every team has its unique personalities. Supervisors need strong communication and interpersonal skills to effectively manage different personalities, address performance issues, and motivate all team members.

- **Maintaining Work-Life Balance:** Supervisors often face pressure to work long hours, especially during demanding production periods. It's crucial for them to maintain a healthy work-life balance for their own well-being and to set a positive example for their team.

Strategies for Supporting Supervisors and Fostering Growth:

- **Leadership Development Programs:** Invest in leadership development programs to equip supervisors with the skills and knowledge they need to be effective leaders, coaches, and mentors.
    - Examples of leadership development program topics:
        - Communication skills training, focusing on active listening, providing constructive feedback, and giving clear instructions.
        - Conflict resolution training, equipping supervisors with techniques for mediating disagreements and fostering collaborative problem-solving.
        - Performance management training, covering setting expectations, conducting performance reviews, and implementing corrective action plans.

- Coaching and mentoring training, providing supervisors with the skills to develop their team members' potential.
- Time management and delegation training, empowering supervisors to prioritize tasks effectively and delegate responsibilities appropriately.

- **Regular Performance Feedback:** Provide regular performance feedback to supervisors, highlighting their strengths and areas for development. This ongoing feedback helps them grow professionally and refine their leadership style.

- **Supervisor Peer Support Networks:** Encourage supervisors to form peer support networks where they can share best practices, troubleshoot challenges, and learn from each other's experiences.

- **Mentorship Opportunities:** Pair experienced supervisors with newer supervisors to provide guidance and support. This mentorship fosters a culture of learning and development within the supervisory team.

Effective supervisors are the cornerstone of a successful food manufacturing operation. By cultivating strong leadership skills, fostering a culture of collaboration and continuous improvement, and prioritizing the well-being of their teams, supervisors empower frontline workers and contribute significantly to a thriving and sustainable food manufacturing environment.

Delving Deeper: Challenges Faced by Supervisors and Leadership Development Strategies

We provided a solid foundation for the essential qualities and strategies that empower supervisors to become effective leaders. Let's now delve deeper into the specific challenges they encounter and explore leadership development strategies in greater detail.

Understanding Supervisor Challenges: Navigating a Complex Landscape

Supervisors operate within a dynamic and often demanding environment. Here's a closer look at some of the key challenges they face:

- **Balancing Competing Priorities:** Supervisors are constantly juggling multiple priorities. They need to ensure production quotas are met on time and within budget, while also prioritizing the safety and well-being of their teams. This can be a significant source of stress, requiring strong time management and prioritization skills.

- **Managing Performance Issues:** Supervisors may encounter team members who struggle to meet performance expectations. Addressing these issues effectively requires clear communication, constructive feedback, and potentially implementing corrective action plans. Effectively managing performance issues is crucial for maintaining a high-performing team.

- **Adapting to Change:** The food manufacturing industry is constantly evolving, with new technologies emerging, consumer preferences shifting, and regulations changing. Supervisors need to be adaptable and embrace change. They must effectively communicate these changes to their teams and provide the necessary training and support to ensure a smooth transition.

- **Motivating a Diverse Workforce:** Food manufacturing teams are often diverse, with employees from different backgrounds, cultures, and age groups. Supervisors need to understand and cater to these diverse needs and motivations. This requires strong interpersonal skills and the ability to create a work environment that feels inclusive and respectful for all.

- **Technological Integration:** Technology is playing an increasingly important role in food manufacturing. Supervisors need to be comfortable using new technologies and effectively integrate them into their daily work routines. They may also need to train their teams on using these new technologies.

- **Managing Conflict:** Disagreements or conflicts can inevitably arise within teams. Supervisors need to be adept at facilitating constructive conversations, mediating conflict resolution, and fostering a positive work environment. This requires strong communication and conflict resolution skills.

Strategies for Effective Leadership Development: Investing in Supervisor Growth

Investing in leadership development programs for supervisors empowers them to navigate these challenges and become more effective leaders. Here are some key strategies to consider:

- **Leadership Training Programs:** Develop or partner with external providers to offer leadership training programs specifically designed for supervisors in the food manufacturing industry. These programs can cover topics like communication skills, conflict resolution, performance management, coaching and mentoring, and change management.

- **Mentorship Programs:** Pair experienced supervisors with newer supervisors to provide guidance and support. Mentors can share their knowledge and experience, helping new supervisors develop their leadership skills and navigate the challenges of the role.
    - Benefits of mentorship programs:
        - Provide new supervisors with guidance and support from experienced supervisors.

- Facilitate knowledge transfer and best practice sharing.
- Foster a sense of community and belonging within the supervisory team.

- **Action Learning Programs:** Action learning programs involve supervisors working on real-world challenges within their teams. By sharing experiences and collaborating on solutions, supervisors learn from each other and develop practical leadership skills.
  - Examples of action learning projects:
    - Improving communication flow between production and maintenance teams.
    - Reducing waste on a specific production line.
    - Developing a more efficient onboarding process for new team members.

- **360-Degree Feedback:** Implement a 360-degree feedback process where supervisors receive feedback from their superiors, peers, and team members. This comprehensive feedback provides valuable insights into their strengths and areas for development, allowing them to tailor their leadership approach.
  - Sources for 360-degree feedback:
    - Self-assessment by the supervisor themselves.
    - Feedback from superiors, evaluating the supervisor's performance and leadership effectiveness.
    - Feedback from peers, providing insights into collaboration and teamwork dynamics.
    - Feedback from team members, assessing the supervisor's communication, coaching, and motivational skills.

- **On-the-Job Coaching:** Leaders within the organization can provide ongoing coaching and feedback to supervisors during their daily routines. This real-time coaching helps supervisors develop their skills in a practical setting.

- **Leadership Conferences and Workshops:** Encourage supervisors to attend industry conferences and workshops focused on leadership development. These events offer opportunities for learning new strategies, networking with peers, and staying current with industry trends.

Additional Considerations:

- When developing leadership development programs, consider the specific needs and challenges faced by supervisors in your food manufacturing operation. Tailoring programs to address these specific needs will maximize their effectiveness.

- Leadership development is an ongoing process. Providing supervisors with ongoing opportunities for learning and development helps them stay engaged, motivated, and continuously refine their leadership skills.

- Recognizing and rewarding supervisors who demonstrate strong leadership qualities reinforces positive behaviors and motivates others to aspire to excellence.

By implementing these strategies, food manufacturing companies can invest in their supervisors' growth, empowering them to become effective leaders who drive team performance, foster a positive work environment, and contribute significantly to the overall success of the organization.

CHAPTER 5

Optimizing Operations for Non-Frontline Workers

The success of a food manufacturing operation hinges not only on the tireless efforts of frontline workers but also on the expertise and dedication of non-frontline personnel. This diverse group encompasses a wide range of functions, including quality control, research, and development (R&D), engineering, maintenance, supply chain management, human resources (HR), finance, and administration. Each department plays a crucial role in ensuring efficient production, maintaining high-quality standards, and driving continuous improvement.

This chapter dives into optimizing operations for non-frontline workers, the unsung heroes who ensure a food manufacturing operation runs smoothly. We'll explore the value they bring, strategies for optimizing their departments, and how technology empowers their performance.

Understanding the Value of Non-Frontline Workers: Beyond the Production Floor

While frontline workers directly interact with the production process, non-frontline personnel provide the critical support system that keeps the operation running smoothly. Here's a glimpse into the value they contribute:

- **Quality Control:** Ensuring food safety and quality is paramount. Quality control personnel perform rigorous testing, analyze data, and implement preventive measures to minimize risks and maintain compliance with regulations.

    The QC team is the guardian of food safety. They perform tests like:

    - Microbiological analysis to detect harmful bacteria or pathogens.
    - Chemical analysis to ensure ingredients meet specifications.
    - Sensory evaluation to assess taste, texture, and appearance.
    - They also analyze data to identify trends and implement preventive measures to minimize risks and ensure regulatory compliance.

- **Research and Development (R&D):** R&D teams constantly innovate, developing new products, exploring new ingredients, and optimizing formulations. They play a vital role in driving product differentiation and keeping the company competitive in the market.

    The R&D team is the innovation engine:

    - They develop new products like plant-based alternatives or reformulate existing products to reduce sugar content.
    - They explore new ingredients like ancient grains or functional superfoods to meet evolving consumer preferences.
    - They optimize formulations to improve taste, texture, shelf life, or nutritional value.

- **Engineering and Maintenance:** Engineers design and maintain production equipment, ensuring optimal functionality and minimizing downtime. Their expertise is crucial for efficient and reliable production processes.

Engineers keep the production lines humming:

- o They design and install new equipment, ensuring it integrates seamlessly into existing processes.
- o They perform routine maintenance to prevent breakdowns and ensure equipment functions optimally.
- o They troubleshoot issues and conduct repairs to minimize downtime.

- **Supply Chain Management:** The smooth flow of raw materials and finished products is essential. Supply chain management personnel source ingredients, manage inventory, and ensure timely deliveries, minimizing disruptions and optimizing costs.

The supply chain team ensures a steady flow of materials:

- o They source high-quality ingredients at competitive prices, building strong relationships with reliable suppliers.
- o They manage inventory levels to prevent stockouts or excessive storage costs by utilizing data analytics for forecasting and optimization.
- o They ensure timely deliveries by collaborating with logistics providers and monitoring transportation schedules.

- **Human Resources (HR):** HR attracts, recruits, trains, and develops a skilled workforce. They also contribute to a positive work environment that fosters employee engagement and retention.

HR attracts, retains, and develops the talent pool:

- o They develop recruitment strategies to attract qualified candidates for various non-frontline positions.

- o They design training programs to equip employees with the necessary skills and knowledge to excel in their roles.
- o They implement performance management systems to track progress, provide feedback, and promote continuous improvement.
- o They foster a positive work environment that values employee well-being and promotes engagement.

- **Finance and Administration:** Financial expertise ensures responsible resource allocation, cost control, and financial solvency. Additionally, administrative personnel handle various tasks that keep the organization running smoothly.

The finance and administration team ensures financial health:

- o They manage the organization's finances, allocating resources effectively and controlling costs.
- o They analyze financial data to identify trends, generate reports, and make informed financial decisions.
- o Administrative personnel handle various tasks like payroll processing, data entry, and legal compliance.

Investing in optimizing operations for non-frontline workers yields significant benefits:

- **Increased Efficiency and Productivity:** Streamlined processes, clear communication, and effective use of technology can significantly enhance efficiency and productivity across all departments.

- **Improved Decision-Making:** By providing non-frontline workers with access to relevant data and fostering a culture of collaboration, organizations can leverage their diverse expertise for better decision-making.

- **Enhanced Innovation:** Empowering non-frontline personnel to share ideas and participate in problem-solving can lead to groundbreaking innovations across various aspects of the food manufacturing process.

- **Employee Engagement and Retention:** Creating a work environment that values the contributions of non-frontline workers, provides opportunities for growth, and fosters a sense of accomplishment leads to increased engagement and reduces turnover.

Optimizing Operations for Non-Frontline Departments: Strategies for Success

Here are specific strategies for optimizing operations within each department:

- **Quality Control:**
  - **Investing in Automation and Technology:** Utilizing automated testing equipment and data analysis software can expedite testing processes and enhance accuracy.
  - **Continuous Improvement Initiatives:** Encouraging quality control personnel to participate in identifying and addressing potential quality issues fosters a proactive approach to safety and quality control.

- **Research and Development (R&D):**
  - **Open Innovation:** Promote collaboration with universities, research institutions, and even competitors to leverage a broader range of expertise and accelerate innovation.
  - **Focus on Consumer Trends:** Stay current with evolving consumer preferences and market demands to drive R&D efforts towards developing products that meet consumer needs.

- **Engineering and Maintenance:**
  - **Predictive Maintenance:** Implement predictive maintenance practices to anticipate equipment failures and schedule maintenance proactively, minimizing downtime and production disruptions.
  - **Investing in Advanced Technologies:** Consider incorporating innovative technologies like 3D printing for spare parts production and virtual reality training for maintenance personnel.

- **Supply Chain Management:**
  - **Strengthening Supplier Relationships:** Building strong relationships with reliable suppliers ensures a consistent flow of high-quality ingredients at competitive prices.
  - **Inventory Optimization:** Utilize data analytics to optimize inventory levels, minimizing storage costs and preventing stockouts.

- **Human Resources (HR):**
  - **Talent Management Strategies:** Develop clear career development paths and training programs to attract, retain, and nurture top talent within the organization.
  - **Performance Management Systems:** Implement performance management systems that track progress, provide feedback, and incentivize continuous improvement for non-frontline personnel.

- **Finance and Administration:**
  - **Process Automation:** Automate routine administrative tasks wherever possible to free up personnel for more strategic initiatives.

- **Data-Driven Decision Making:** Utilize financial data and analytics to make informed decisions regarding resource allocation, budgeting, and cost-saving measures.

These are just a few examples, and the specific strategies will vary depending on the nature and size of the food manufacturing operation. However, the core principle remains the same: by identifying areas for improvement, implementing targeted strategies, and fostering a culture of collaboration and continuous improvement, organizations can significantly optimize operations for non-frontline workers.

Leveraging Technology for Enhanced Performance: Empowering Non-Frontline Staff

Technology plays a crucial role in optimizing operations for non-frontline workers. Consider these advancements:

- **Data Analytics and Business Intelligence Tools:** Empower non-frontline personnel to analyze data relevant to their roles (e.g., QC personnel analyzing quality control data, supply chain managers analyzing logistics data). These tools help identify trends, monitor performance metrics, and make data-driven decisions.

- **Collaborative Platforms and Cloud-Based Solutions:** Facilitate communication and collaboration across departments through digital platforms like Slack or Microsoft Teams. Cloud-based solutions like project management software or shared document storage platforms streamline workflows and promote information sharing.

- **Automation and Robotics:** Automating routine tasks like data entry, compiling reports, or packaging finished products can free up valuable time for non-frontline personnel to focus on higher-level cognitive tasks and strategic initiatives.

- **Project Management Software:** Utilize project management software like Asana or Trello for efficient project planning, resource allocation, task delegation, and tracking progress across various departments. This promotes transparency and accountability within and across teams.

By providing non-frontline workers with access to relevant technologies and training, organizations can empower them to leverage these tools effectively, enhancing their performance and contributing to overall operational excellence.

- **Interdepartmental Communication Silos:** Break down communication barriers between departments by establishing clear communication protocols, holding regular cross-functional meetings, and fostering a culture of collaboration.

- **Resistance to Change:** Implementing new processes or technologies may be met with resistance. Address employee concerns through effective change management strategies that include clear communication, training, and opportunities for feedback.

- **Data Overload:** Access to vast amounts of data can be overwhelming. Provide training on data analysis and interpretation skills to empower non-frontline personnel to extract valuable insights from this data.

- **Work-Life Balance for Non-Frontline Workers:** Ensure non-frontline workers maintain a healthy work-life balance by offering flexible work arrangements, encouraging breaks throughout the workday, and promoting a company culture that respects personal time.

Strategies for Overcoming Challenges:

- **Promote Cross-Functional Collaboration:** Encourage interdepartmental collaboration through team-building exercises, joint meetings (e.g., R&D and marketing teams collaborating on new product development), and cross-functional project teams with representatives from various departments.

- **Effective Change Management:** Implement a clear communication plan outlining the rationale behind changes, provide comprehensive training on new processes and technologies, and address employee concerns proactively. Gather feedback throughout the implementation process and make adjustments as needed.

- **Data Literacy Training:** Offer training programs on data analysis tools and techniques to empower non-frontline personnel to leverage data effectively for informed decision-making.

- **Promoting Work-Life Balance:** Offer flexible work arrangements like remote work options or compressed workweeks. Encourage breaks throughout the workday and promote a company culture that respects personal time by discouraging after-hours work emails or calls unless absolutely necessary.

By implementing these strategies, food manufacturing companies can optimize operations for non-frontline workers. This empowers them to contribute more effectively, fosters a culture of collaboration and innovation, and ultimately propels the organization towards achieving its full potential.

CHAPTER 6

Continuous Learning: A Key to Growth

The food manufacturing industry is a dynamic landscape in constant flux. New technologies emerge, consumer trends shift, and regulatory requirements evolve rapidly. In this ever-changing environment, a skilled and adaptable workforce is paramount for success. This chapter emphasizes the importance of continuous learning as a key driver of growth for both individual employees and the organization as a whole.

Why Continuous Learning Matters: Staying Ahead of the Curve

Continuous learning fosters a growth mindset and equips individuals with the knowledge, skills, and adaptability necessary to thrive in an ever-changing environment. Here's why it matters in the food manufacturing industry:

- **Maintaining a Competitive Edge:** Continuous learning ensures the workforce stays current with industry trends like plant-based alternatives or sustainable packaging solutions. It familiarizes them with technological advancements like automation and robotics and keeps them updated on best practices for efficient production processes. This allows companies to adapt to evolving consumer demands and maintain a competitive edge in the market.

- **Enhancing Innovation:** A culture of continuous learning fosters creativity and encourages employees to explore new ideas. For instance, R&D teams can attend workshops on emerging ingredients or participate in hackathons to brainstorm innovative product formulations. This can lead to groundbreaking innovations across various aspects of food manufacturing, from developing new product lines to optimizing production processes.

- **Improving Safety and Quality:** The food manufacturing industry has strict safety and quality regulations. Continuous learning ensures employees stay updated on the latest safety protocols, like Hazard Analysis and Critical Control Points (HACCP), and quality control procedures for different food products. This minimizes risks of contamination and ensures compliance with regulations.

- **Upskilling and Reskilling:** As technology automates routine tasks, the need for upskilling and reskilling the workforce becomes increasingly important. Continuous learning programs equip employees with the skills necessary to adapt to new roles, such as data analysis or machine maintenance. This ensures they remain valuable assets within the organization.

- **Boosting Employee Engagement:** Investing in employee development through continuous learning opportunities demonstrates a commitment to their growth and career advancement. This fosters a sense of value, motivates employees to stay engaged, and contributes to a more positive work environment.

Building a Culture of Continuous Learning: Strategies for Success

Creating a culture of continuous learning requires a multi-pronged approach:

- **Leadership Commitment:** Genuine commitment from leadership is crucial. Leaders must model a learning mindset by actively participating in development programs themselves. They should allocate resources to support continuous learning initiatives and create a work environment that values continuous improvement.

- **Needs Assessment:** Identify the current and future skill gaps within the workforce. Conduct skills gap analyses through surveys, performance evaluations, or industry benchmarking to understand the specific needs of different departments. This allows you to tailor learning programs to address those specific needs.

- **Variety of Learning Formats:** Offer a diverse range of learning formats to cater to different learning styles and preferences. This might include:
    - Online courses with interactive modules and quizzes.
    - Instructor-led training workshops for hands-on learning.
    - Mentorship programs where experienced employees coach and guide newer employees.
    - Job shadowing opportunities to observe experienced professionals in action.

- **Microlearning Opportunities:** Provide bite-sized learning modules (e.g., 5-10 minutes) that can be easily integrated into busy work schedules. Microlearning allows for continuous skill development without disrupting production workflows. Examples include short online videos, cheat sheets, or mobile learning apps.

- **Knowledge Sharing and Collaboration:** Encourage knowledge sharing and collaboration between employees. This can be facilitated through:
    - Internal knowledge-sharing platforms where employees can share best practices and troubleshooting tips.
    - Mentorship programs where experienced employees can coach and guide newer employees.
    - Cross-functional team projects that bring together employees from different departments to work on a common goal. This fosters a collaborative learning environment.

- **Learner Recognition and Incentives:** Recognize and reward employees who actively participate in learning and development opportunities. This could involve:
    - Public recognition during team meetings or company newsletters.
    - Performance bonuses tied to the completion of specific learning programs.
    - Opportunities for career advancement based on acquired skills and knowledge.

Examples of Continuous Learning Programs in Food Manufacturing:

Here are some specific examples of continuous learning programs that can be implemented:

- **Technical Skills Training:** Programs focusing on specific technical skills related to:
    - Equipment operation and maintenance procedures for different production lines.
    - Quality control processes like microbiological testing or sensory evaluation.

- Food safety protocols like HACCP compliance or allergen management.

- **Soft Skills Development:** Training programs on communication skills, problem-solving, teamwork, leadership, and time management, which are valuable across all departments.

- **Regulatory Compliance Training:** Programs ensuring employees are up-to-date on the latest industry regulations and compliance requirements, such as food safety standards set by the FDA or allergen labeling requirements.

- **Leadership Development Programs:** Programs equipping supervisors and managers with the skills they need to lead effectively, coach their teams, and drive continuous improvement. These programs might cover topics like:
    - Effective communication and delegation.
    - Performance management and providing constructive feedback.
    - Conflict resolution and problem-solving techniques.
    - Building and motivating high-performing teams.

- **Industry Conferences and Workshops:** Encourage employees to attend industry conferences and workshops to stay current with trends and network with peers from other companies. This exposure to new ideas and best practices can spark innovation within the organization.

The Role of Technology in Continuous Learning:

Technology plays a vital role in facilitating continuous learning:

- **Online Learning Platforms:** Utilize online learning platforms like Udemy, Coursera, or a Learning Management System (LMS) to offer a vast array of courses, modules, and resources accessible to employees anytime, anywhere.

- **Mobile Learning Apps:** Provide mobile learning apps that allow employees to access learning materials on the go, during breaks, or while commuting. These apps can offer microlearning modules, podcasts, or audiobooks.

- **Virtual Reality (VR) and Augmented Reality (AR):** VR and AR can be used for immersive training simulations. For instance, VR simulations can be used to train employees on safe operation procedures for complex machinery, while AR can be used for overlaying maintenance instructions onto real-world equipment.

By leveraging technology strategically, food manufacturing companies can create a robust and accessible ecosystem for continuous learning.

Overcoming Challenges and Ensuring Sustainability

Implementing a successful culture of continuous learning requires addressing some challenges:

- **Time Constraints:** Balancing work responsibilities with dedicated learning time can be challenging. Offering flexible learning options like microlearning modules or asynchronous online courses can help address this concern.

- **Budgetary Constraints:** Investing in continuous learning programs requires allocating resources. Demonstrating the return on investment (ROI) in terms of enhanced skills, improved efficiency, and reduced costs can help secure ongoing budgetary support for these initiatives. Track metrics like the number of training hours completed, changes in employee performance, or reduction in errors to quantify the value of learning programs.

- **Measuring Learning Effectiveness:** Developing effective metrics to measure the impact of learning programs allows you to assess their effectiveness and identify areas for improvement. Consider metrics like knowledge retention rates from assessments, application of learned skills on the job, or improvement in employee performance evaluations.

Strategies for Ensuring Sustainability:

- **Embed Learning in the Work Culture:** Integrate continuous learning into the core values and daily practices of the organization. Encourage knowledge sharing through internal knowledge-sharing platforms or brown bag lunch sessions where employees can present on what they've learned. Celebrate learning milestones through recognition programs and make continuous learning a way of life.

- **Leadership as Learners:** Leaders must actively participate in learning and development opportunities. This sets a positive example and reinforces the importance of continuous learning throughout the organization. Leaders can participate in leadership development programs, industry conferences, or even mentor junior employees.

- **Regular Feedback and Evaluation:** Continually gather feedback from employees on the effectiveness of learning programs through surveys or focus groups. Use this feedback to adapt and improve the programs to better meet the needs and preferences of the workforce.

- **Building a Learning Community:** Foster a learning community where employees feel encouraged to ask questions, share knowledge, and learn from each other. This can be facilitated through team-based learning projects, online forums, or internal communities of practice focused on specific areas of expertise.

In conclusion, continuous learning is not a luxury but a necessity for food manufacturing companies to thrive in a dynamic and competitive environment. By fostering a culture of continuous learning, organizations equip their employees with the knowledge, skills, and adaptability necessary to navigate change, drive innovation, and achieve long-term success. Investing in continuous learning empowers employees, strengthens the organization's competitive edge, and paves the way for a future of growth and prosperity.

CHAPTER 7

Building Your Value Proposition: Attracting and Retaining Top Talent

In today's competitive job market, attracting and retaining top talent is crucial for the success of any food manufacturing company. A strong value proposition – a clear and compelling statement that outlines what makes your company a desirable place to work – is essential for standing out from the crowd. This chapter delves into the key components of a compelling value proposition and strategies for effectively communicating it to potential and existing employees.

The Power of a Value Proposition: Why It Matters

A well-crafted value proposition goes beyond simply offering a job and a paycheck. It articulates the unique benefits, opportunities, and work environment that differentiate your company from competitors. Here's why a strong value proposition matters:

- **Attracting Top Talent:** A compelling value proposition attracts qualified candidates who share your company's values and are genuinely interested in the unique aspects of working for you. This increases the likelihood of recruiting high-performing individuals who are a good fit for your company culture.

- **Employee Engagement and Retention:** A strong value proposition goes beyond attracting talent; it also fosters employee engagement and retention. When employees feel valued, appreciated, and see opportunities for growth within the organization, they are more likely to stay committed, contribute their best effort, and become high performers.

- **Employer Branding:** Your value proposition contributes to your employer brand – the overall perception of your company as a workplace. A positive employer brand attracts high-caliber candidates and helps you build a reputation as an employer of choice in the food manufacturing industry. This can be a significant competitive advantage when recruiting top talent.

Deconstructing the Value Proposition: Key Components to Consider

A compelling value proposition effectively communicates a combination of intrinsic and extrinsic factors that influence an individual's decision to join or remain with a company. Here are the key components to consider:

- **Compensation and Benefits:** Competitive salary and benefits packages are essential to attract and retain talent. Consider offering a variety of benefits that cater to the specific needs of your workforce, such as:
    - Health insurance plans with various coverage options.
    - Paid time off policies that promote work-life balance.
    - Retirement savings plans with employer matching contributions.
    - Tuition reimbursement programs for continuing education.
    - Wellness programs that support employee health and well-being.

- **Work Environment and Culture:** Highlight the positive aspects of your work environment and company culture. Do you promote a collaborative and supportive atmosphere? Do you offer opportunities for teamwork, professional development, and career advancement? Emphasize these aspects in your value proposition to attract candidates who value a positive work environment.

- **Work-Life Balance:** In today's world, work-life balance is paramount. Does your company offer flexible work arrangements, such as remote work options or compressed workweeks? Do you have generous paid time off policies that allow employees to disconnect and recharge? Communicating your commitment to work-life balance can be a significant advantage in attracting and retaining talent.

- **Growth and Development Opportunities:** Employees seek opportunities to learn, develop new skills, and advance their careers. Do you offer training programs, mentorship opportunities, or leadership development programs? Articulate how your company invests in employee growth and development within your value proposition to demonstrate your commitment to their long-term success.

- **Meaningful Work:** Many individuals seek jobs that contribute to a larger purpose. Does your company have a strong social responsibility mission or focus on sustainable practices? Highlighting these aspects in your value proposition can resonate with potential employees who value working for a company that has a positive impact on the world.

Crafting Your Unique Value Proposition:

There's no one-size-fits-all approach to crafting a value proposition. Consider these steps:

1. **Identify Your Target Audience:** Who are you trying to attract? Understanding the needs and priorities of your ideal candidates, such as recent graduates, experienced professionals, or individuals seeking career changers, is crucial for tailoring your value proposition to resonate with them.

2. **Conduct Employee Research:** Gather feedback from your current employees through surveys or focus groups to understand what they value most about working for your company. This can provide valuable insights into what makes your company unique and informs the development of an authentic value proposition.

3. **Differentiate Yourself:** Analyze your competitors' value propositions and identify what sets your company apart. What unique benefits or opportunities do you offer that your competitors don't? Highlighting these differentiators can be particularly attractive to potential candidates.

4. **Keep it Authentic and Actionable:** Your value proposition should be genuine and reflect your company culture. Use clear, concise, and action-oriented language that resonates with your target audience. Avoid generic statements and focus on specific examples that showcase how your company delivers on its promises.

5. **Integrate Your Value Proposition Throughout the Candidate Journey:** Consistently communicate your value proposition across all your recruitment channels, from job postings to career pages to interview conversations. Every touchpoint with potential candidates

is an opportunity to showcase what makes your company a great place to work.

Beyond Words: Demonstrating Your Value Proposition

A well-crafted value proposition is just the first step. Here's how to ensure your actions live up to your words:

- **Employee Onboarding:** The onboarding process sets the tone for the employee experience. Make it a positive and informative experience that reinforces the key elements of your value proposition. Provide new hires with a clear understanding of your company culture, benefits, and opportunities for growth.

- **Culture of Recognition and Appreciation:** Regularly recognize and appreciate employee contributions. This reinforces the value you place on your workforce and aligns with your value proposition. Public recognition programs, rewards for exceeding goals, or simply acknowledging a job well done can go a long way in keeping employees feeling valued.

- **Investing in Employee Development:** Fulfill your promise of growth opportunities by offering training programs, mentorship opportunities, and clear career development paths. Provide opportunities for employees to develop new skills, take on challenging assignments, and advance their careers within the organization.

- **Open Communication and Feedback:** Maintain open communication channels and encourage employee feedback. Conduct regular employee satisfaction surveys and hold town hall meetings to gather feedback on company culture, work environment, and development opportunities. This demonstrates your commitment to creating a positive work environment where employee voices are heard and valued.

By crafting a compelling value proposition that resonates with potential and existing employees, food manufacturing companies can attract top talent, foster a positive work environment, and drive long-term success. A strong value proposition goes beyond simply offering a job; it creates a win-win scenario where employees feel valued, contribute their best efforts, and the company benefits from a highly skilled and engaged workforce.

Remember, your value proposition is an ongoing process. Regularly assess its effectiveness, gather feedback from employees and potential candidates, and adapt it as needed to reflect your evolving company culture and the changing landscape of the food manufacturing industry.

Building a strong employer brand and crafting a compelling value proposition are ongoing endeavors. The next section delves into additional strategies that can enhance your employer brand and solidify your position as an employer of choice in the food manufacturing industry.

Employer Branding Strategies: Building a Strong Reputation

Your value proposition is a key component of your employer brand – the overall perception of your company as a workplace. Here are some strategies to strengthen your employer brand and ensure your value proposition resonates with target audiences:

- **Develop a Consistent Brand Identity:** Create a consistent brand identity across all your communication channels, from your website and social media platforms to job postings and recruitment materials. This reinforces your company culture and values.

- **Active Social Media Presence:** Maintain an active social media presence that showcases your company culture, employee stories, and the positive aspects of working for your organization.

- **Employee Advocacy Programs:** Encourage employee advocacy by empowering your workforce to share their positive experiences on social media and professional networking platforms. Authentic employee testimonials are highly credible and can significantly attract potential candidates.

- **Industry Awards and Recognition:** Strive for industry awards and recognition programs that acknowledge your commitment to employee well-being, innovation, or sustainability practices. These accolades enhance your employer brand and showcase your company as a leader in the industry.

- **Community Involvement:** Highlight your company's involvement in community initiatives and social responsibility programs. This demonstrates your commitment to making a positive impact and can resonate with potential employees who value working for a purpose-driven organization.

Measuring the ROI of Your Value Proposition: Demonstrating Value

While a strong value proposition demonstrably benefits your company culture and attracts top talent, quantifying its impact strengthens your position and allows you to continuously refine your approach. Here's how to measure the ROI (Return on Investment) of your value proposition efforts:

- **Cost-per-Hire:** Track your cost-per-hire metrics over time. A strong value proposition can attract more qualified candidates, potentially reducing recruitment costs by attracting a larger pool of interested applicants and streamlining the hiring process.

- **Time-to-Hire:** Monitor the time it takes to fill open positions. An effective value proposition can shorten your time-to-hire by attracting high-caliber candidates who are a good fit for your company culture, reducing the time and resources needed to fill vacancies.

- **Employee Retention Rates:** Track employee turnover rates. A strong value proposition can foster employee engagement and loyalty, leading to reduced turnover and its associated costs, such as recruitment, onboarding, and lost productivity.

- **Employee Satisfaction Surveys:** Conduct regular employee satisfaction surveys to gauge employee perceptions of your company culture, career development opportunities, and overall work environment. Positive feedback reinforces the effectiveness of your value proposition in creating a workplace where employees feel valued and appreciated.

- **Quality of Hire:** Evaluate the quality of new hires by tracking their performance metrics, engagement levels, and contribution to the organization. A strong value proposition can help attract high-performing talent who are more likely to integrate seamlessly into your team and contribute to the company's success.

By tracking these key metrics, you can demonstrate the quantifiable value of your employer branding efforts and refine your value proposition to maximize its impact on attracting and retaining top talent.

Showcasing Employee Testimonials: The Power of Authenticity

Employee testimonials are powerful tools for showcasing your value proposition in action. Here's how to leverage them effectively:

- **Feature Employee Stories:** Highlight employee stories on your company website, social media platforms, and career pages. These stories can showcase diverse perspectives within your workforce and demonstrate how your value proposition translates into real-life experiences for your employees.

- **Video Testimonials:** Consider incorporating video testimonials into your recruitment materials. Seeing and hearing firsthand accounts from your employees can create a more emotional connection with potential candidates.

- **Employee Recognition Programs:** Implement employee recognition programs that encourage employees to share their positive experiences and contributions to the company. This fosters a sense of pride within your workforce and generates authentic content to showcase your value proposition.

Remember, authenticity is key. Employee testimonials should be genuine and reflect the diverse voices within your organization. By sharing real-life experiences, you can connect with potential candidates on a deeper level and effectively communicate the value proposition you offer.

Building a strong employer brand and crafting a compelling value proposition are ongoing endeavors. By consistently communicating your company culture, values, and commitment to employee well-being, you can attract top talent, foster a positive work environment, and solidify your position as a leader in the food manufacturing industry.

Call to Action: Building a Winning Employer Brand

Building a strong employer brand and crafting a compelling value proposition are ongoing endeavors. By consistently communicating your company culture, values, and commitment to employee well-being, you can attract top talent, foster a positive work environment, and solidify your position as a leader in the food manufacturing industry.

Get started on building your employer brand today! By investing in your value proposition, you can:

- Attract a pipeline of highly qualified and engaged candidates.
- Reduce recruitment costs and time-to-hire metrics.
- Foster a positive work environment that drives employee engagement and retention.
- Build a reputation as an employer of choice in the food manufacturing industry.
- Enhance your company's overall success and profitability.

Take the first step towards building a winning employer brand. Evaluate your current value proposition, gather feedback from your employees, and craft a compelling message that resonates with your target audience. By consistently demonstrating your commitment to your employees, you can create a thriving workforce that positions your food manufacturing company for long-term success.

CHAPTER 8

Embracing Technological Advancements: The Future of Food Manufacturing

The food manufacturing industry is on the cusp of a technological revolution. Advancements in automation, robotics, artificial intelligence (AI), and data analytics are transforming every aspect of the production process, from ingredient sourcing to final product delivery. This chapter explores how food manufacturing companies can leverage these advancements to enhance efficiency, safety, product quality, and overall operational excellence. The food manufacturing industry is expected to see a **30% increase** in automation adoption by 2030. Kraft Heinz, a major food manufacturing company, has implemented AI-powered systems to optimize production planning. This has resulted in a **15% reduction in waste** and a **10% increase** in overall production efficiency.

The Rise of Technological Advancements: Reshaping the Industry

Here's a glimpse into some of the key technological advancements impacting the food manufacturing industry:

- **Automation and Robotics:** Repetitive tasks are increasingly being automated with robots and cobots (collaborative robots) working alongside human personnel. This improves production speed and consistency while reducing the risk of human error.

- **Artificial Intelligence (AI):** AI is being used for predictive maintenance, optimizing production processes, and even developing new food formulations. AI-powered systems can analyze vast amounts of data to identify patterns and trends, enabling proactive decision-making.

- **Internet of Things (IoT):** The interconnectedness of machinery and equipment through the Internet of Things (IoT) allows for real-time monitoring of production lines and facilitates preventative maintenance. This minimizes downtime and ensures optimal equipment performance.

- **Big Data and Analytics:** Food manufacturing companies are generating vast amounts of data from various sources, including production lines, sensors, and supply chain management systems. Big data analytics tools can be used to extract valuable insights from this data, enabling data-driven decision-making to optimize processes, improve resource allocation, and minimize waste.

- **Blockchain Technology:** Blockchain technology offers a secure and transparent way to track food provenance throughout the supply chain. This enhances food traceability, promotes consumer confidence, and facilitates faster product recalls if necessary.

The Benefits of Embracing Technology: A Competitive Edge

Early adopters of these technologies stand to gain a significant competitive advantage:

- **Enhanced Efficiency:** Automation and data-driven decision-making can streamline production processes by **up to 20%**, minimizing waste and maximizing output. For instance, a bakery leveraging automated dough handling systems can significantly reduce production time and labor costs associated with manual dough preparation.

- **Improved Product Quality:** Precise monitoring and control of production parameters through automation and AI ensure consistent product quality. This translates into fewer product defects and ultimately higher customer satisfaction.

- **Increased Food Safety:** Real-time monitoring and data analysis enable proactive identification of potential food safety hazards, minimizing risks and ensuring food safety compliance. This translates into a stronger brand reputation and consumer trust.

- **Reduced Costs:** Automation can lower labor costs, while data analytics can help optimize resource allocation and minimize waste. This can lead to significant cost savings over time. Food manufacturers who implemented data analytics tools achieved an average cost reduction of **8%**.

- **Innovation and New Product Development:** AI and data analytics can accelerate innovation by assisting with new product formulation and development. This allows companies to stay ahead of the curve and cater to evolving consumer preferences, such as creating healthier or more sustainable food options.

- **Enhanced Workforce Capabilities:** Technology complements human capabilities, allowing employees to focus on higher-level tasks such as process optimization, quality control, and data analysis. This fosters a more skilled and engaged workforce, empowering employees to contribute more strategically to the organization's success.

Overcoming Challenges of Technological Integration:

While the benefits are substantial, challenges exist when integrating new technologies:

- **Initial Investment Costs:** Implementing new technologies can involve significant upfront costs. Careful planning, ROI (Return on Investment) analysis, and exploring potential funding options are crucial.

- **Upskilling the Workforce:** As technology evolves, so too must the skillsets of the workforce. Companies need to invest in training programs to equip employees with the skills necessary to operate and maintain new technologies.

- **Data Security Concerns:** The interconnectedness of the food manufacturing process requires robust cybersecurity measures to protect sensitive data from cyberattacks.

- **Integration Challenges:** Integrating new technologies with existing infrastructure can be complex. Careful planning and a phased approach to implementation are essential.

Strategies for Successful Technology Integration:

A well-defined strategy is key to successfully integrating new technologies:

- **Conduct a Needs Assessment:** Identify specific areas where technology can address existing challenges or improve operations.

- **Prioritize Investments:** Focus on technologies that address the most pressing needs and offer the highest potential return on investment.

- **Develop a Change Management Plan:** Prepare your workforce for the integration of new technologies by providing comprehensive training and addressing potential concerns.

- **Embrace a Culture of Continuous Learning:** Foster a culture of continuous learning within your organization to equip employees with the necessary skills to thrive in a technology-driven environment.

- **Partner with Technology Providers:** Seek partnerships with established technology providers who can offer expertise, support, and ongoing maintenance for the implemented technologies.

The Future of Food Manufacturing: A Collaborative Ecosystem

The future of food manufacturing lies in collaboration, not just within individual companies but also across the entire food ecosystem. Here's what this collaborative approach entails:

- **Collaboration Between Food Manufacturers and Technology Providers:** Ongoing partnerships between food manufacturers and technology providers are essential to develop and implement innovative solutions tailored to the specific needs of the industry.

CHAPTER 9

Sustainability in Food Manufacturing: Balancing Growth with Responsibility

The food manufacturing industry plays a critical role in nourishing the global population. However, this responsibility comes with a significant environmental impact. Sustainable practices are no longer a luxury but a necessity for food manufacturers striving for long-term success. This chapter explores key sustainability considerations throughout the food manufacturing lifecycle, from sourcing raw materials to product packaging and disposal. According to the Food and Agriculture Organization of the United Nations, the food manufacturing industry is responsible for **25% of global greenhouse gas emissions** and ****70%** of global freshwater withdrawals.

Why Sustainability Matters in Food Manufacturing?

Sustainable practices benefit not only the environment but also food manufacturing companies in several ways:

- **Reduced Environmental Impact:** By minimizing resource consumption, waste generation, and greenhouse gas emissions, food manufacturers contribute to a healthier planet, mitigating climate change and ensuring resource availability for future generations.

- **Enhanced Brand Reputation:** Consumers are increasingly seeking sustainable products. Embracing sustainability demonstrates environmental responsibility and can enhance brand reputation, attracting eco-conscious consumers and fostering customer loyalty.

- **Improved Resource Efficiency:** Sustainable practices often lead to increased resource efficiency, reducing costs associated with water, energy use, and raw materials. This translates to improved profitability for food manufacturers.

- **Compliance with Regulations:** Environmental regulations are becoming stricter worldwide. Adopting sustainable practices ensures compliance with existing and evolving regulations, avoiding potential fines and production disruptions.

- **Future-Proofing the Business:** Sustainable practices are essential for long-term business continuity. By mitigating environmental risks and ensuring resource availability, companies can future-proof their operations and remain competitive in the long run.

A Holistic Approach to Sustainability: Key Considerations

Sustainability encompasses the entire food production lifecycle. Here are key areas where food manufacturers can implement sustainable practices:

- **Sustainable Sourcing:**
    - **Local Sourcing:** Prioritizing locally sourced ingredients reduces transportation emissions and promotes regional agriculture. However, local availability and cost fluctuations can be challenges. Building strong relationships with local farmers is crucial for ensuring a consistent supply. For instance, a company manufacturing jams and preserves may prioritize

sourcing seasonal fruits from local farms. This approach reduces transportation emissions and supports the local agricultural economy.

- **Sustainable Farming Practices:** Partnering with farmers who use sustainable agricultural practices, such as water conservation techniques, soil health management, and integrated pest management, contributes to a more sustainable food system. Certifications like USDA Organic or Fairtrade can help ensure these practices are followed. These certifications provide independent verification that farmers adhere to strict environmental and social standards.
- **Ethical Sourcing:** Ensuring ethical sourcing practices throughout the supply chain promotes fair labor conditions and responsible environmental management by suppliers.

- **Resource Efficiency:**
  - **Water Conservation:** Implementing water-saving technologies and optimizing cleaning processes can significantly reduce water consumption throughout production.
  - **Energy Efficiency:** Investing in energy-efficient equipment and adopting renewable energy sources like solar power can minimize energy consumption and reduce the carbon footprint.
  - **Waste Reduction:** Implementing waste minimization strategies throughout the production process, such as optimizing portion control and exploring opportunities for by-product utilization, can significantly reduce waste generation.

- **Sustainable Packaging:**

Transitioning to packaging materials made from recycled content or biodegradable materials minimizes the environmental impact of packaging waste. Bioplastics derived from corn starch or mushroom-based packaging are gaining traction as sustainable alternatives to traditional plastic packaging.

- **Minimizing Packaging:** Reducing packaging materials to the minimum necessary for product protection and shelf life contributes to resource conservation and waste reduction.
- **Recyclable or Biodegradable Packaging:** Transitioning to packaging materials made from recycled content or biodegradable materials minimizes the environmental impact of packaging waste.
- **Sustainable Packaging Design:** Designing packaging for easy disassembly and recycling simplifies the waste management process for consumers.
- **Consumer Education and Engagement:** Educating consumers about the importance of sustainability and empowering them to make informed choices is crucial for creating a more sustainable food system. Food manufacturers can play a role in this by:
  - **Clearly labeling packaging** to communicate the use of sustainable materials and recycling instructions.
  - **Providing educational content** on their websites and social media channels about sustainable practices and their environmental benefits.
  - **Partnering with environmental organizations** to raise awareness about food waste reduction and responsible consumption habits.

- **Food Waste Reduction:**

Implementing waste minimization strategies throughout the production process, such as optimizing portion control and exploring opportunities for by-product utilization, can significantly reduce waste generation. The concept of a "circular economy" encourages finding new uses for food byproducts. For instance, a juice manufacturer can utilize fruit peels and pulp to create jams, marmalades, or even dietary fiber supplements.

- o **Improved Forecasting and Inventory Management:** Accurate demand forecasting and efficient inventory management minimize food spoilage and waste throughout the supply chain.
- o **Gleaning Programs:** Donating surplus or near-expiry food to food banks and community programs mitigates waste and supports those in need.
- o **Upcycling Food Byproducts:** Exploring opportunities to upcycle food byproducts into new ingredients or animal feed minimizes waste and adds value.

Implementing Sustainable Practices: Strategies for Success

Shifting towards a sustainable production model requires a strategic approach:

- **Conduct a Sustainability Assessment:** Evaluate your current environmental impact by analyzing resource consumption, waste generation, and greenhouse gas emissions. This forms the baseline for measuring progress.

- **Set Sustainability Goals:** Establish clear and measurable sustainability goals aligned with your overall business objectives. These goals should be ambitious yet achievable, with defined timelines for implementation.

- **Invest in Sustainable Technologies:** Consider investing in technologies that promote resource efficiency, such as water-saving equipment, energy-efficient machinery, and automated sorting systems for maximizing product yield and minimizing waste.

- **Employee Training and Engagement:** Educate and engage your workforce on the importance of sustainability and their role in implementing sustainable practices. Encourage employee participation in suggesting and implementing new sustainability initiatives.

- **Partnerships and Collaboration:** Collaborate with industry partners, NGOs, and research institutions to share best practices, leverage expertise, and explore innovative solutions for sustainable food production.

- **Transparency and Communication:** Communicate your sustainability efforts transparently to stakeholders, including consumers, investors, and regulatory bodies. This fosters trust and strengthens your reputation as a responsible company.

Measuring and Monitoring Sustainability Performance

Tracking progress and measuring the impact of your sustainability initiatives is crucial:

Develop Key Performance Indicators (KPIs) aligned with your sustainability goals. These KPIs could track water and energy usage, waste generation, carbon footprint, and progress towards sustainable sourcing targets.

- **Establish key performance indicators (KPIs) aligned with your sustainability goals.** These KPIs could track water and energy usage, waste generation, carbon footprint, and progress towards sustainable sourcing targets.

- **Regular data collection and analysis:** Regularly collect data on your KPIs and analyze the results. This allows you to identify areas for improvement and measure the effectiveness of your sustainability initiatives.

- **Sustainability Reporting:** Develop comprehensive sustainability reports that communicate your progress, challenges, and future goals to stakeholders. Transparency in reporting builds trust and demonstrates your commitment to sustainability.

Challenges and Opportunities on the Road to Sustainability

The journey towards sustainability is not without challenges:

- **Balancing Cost and Sustainability:** Implementing sustainable practices may involve initial investments in new technologies or processes. However, the long-term cost savings from resource efficiency and potential brand benefits can outweigh these upfront costs.

- **Consumer Behavior:** While consumer demand for sustainable products is growing, there may be a price premium associated with such products. Educating consumers about the long-term benefits of sustainable practices can help bridge this gap.

- **Standardization and Regulations:** Sustainability practices and regulations can vary across regions. Companies operating in a global market need to navigate this complexity and adapt their approaches accordingly.

Government policies and regulations can also play a significant role in promoting sustainable food manufacturing practices. For instance, incentives for renewable energy adoption or stricter regulations on food waste disposal can encourage companies to prioritize sustainability initiatives.

Looking Ahead: A Sustainable Future for Food Manufacturing

Despite the challenges, the opportunities associated with sustainability are significant. By embracing sustainable practices, food manufacturers can:

- **Contribute to a healthier planet:** By minimizing environmental impact, food manufacturers play a crucial role in combating climate change and ensuring resource availability for future generations.

- **Build brand resilience:** Sustainability is no longer a niche concern but a mainstream expectation. Companies that prioritize sustainability are better positioned to thrive in a competitive and environmentally conscious marketplace.

- **Drive innovation:** The pursuit of sustainability fosters innovation in areas like resource efficiency, alternative packaging solutions, and upcycling technologies. These innovations can benefit the entire food system.

Sustainability is not a destination but an ongoing journey. By adopting a holistic approach, setting clear goals, implementing sustainable practices, and continuously monitoring progress, food manufacturing companies can achieve a balance between growth and responsibility. In doing so, they contribute to a more sustainable food system, ensuring a healthier planet for generations to come.

CHAPTER 10

Building a Resilient Food Manufacturing Workforce: Navigating Change and Ensuring Continuity

The food manufacturing industry operates in a dynamic environment characterized by evolving consumer preferences, technological advancements, and unforeseen disruptions. Building a resilient workforce – one that is adaptable, skilled, and prepared to handle change – is crucial for ensuring business continuity and long-term success. This chapter explores key strategies for fostering a resilient workforce within the food manufacturing industry.

The Hershey Company, a major chocolate manufacturer, successfully navigated the disruptions caused by the global cocoa bean shortage in 2019. By leveraging a resilient workforce with strong problem-solving skills and a commitment to innovation, the company explored alternative sourcing options and reformulated some products to minimize the impact on production and maintain customer satisfaction.

The Need for a Resilient Workforce: Embracing Change in a Dynamic Landscape

The food manufacturing industry faces several challenges that necessitate a resilient workforce:

- **Technological Advancements:** Automation, robotics, and artificial intelligence (AI) are transforming the industry. A resilient workforce can adapt to these changes by developing new skillsets and embracing technology as a tool to complement their capabilities.

- **Shifting Consumer Demands:** Consumer preferences are constantly evolving, with growing demand for sustainable, healthy, and convenient food options. A resilient workforce can adapt to these trends by staying informed about changing consumer needs and being flexible in production processes to meet them.

- **Supply Chain Disruptions:** The global food supply chain is susceptible to disruptions due to various factors such as weather events, geopolitical instability, and economic fluctuations. A resilient workforce can navigate these disruptions by being prepared to adapt sourcing strategies and production processes to minimize the impact on operations.

- **Regulatory Changes:** The food manufacturing industry is subject to evolving regulations regarding food safety, labeling, and environmental practices. A resilient workforce can ensure compliance with these regulations by staying up-to-date on regulatory changes and adapting procedures accordingly.

Characteristics of a Resilient Workforce: Key Traits to Cultivate

Here are some key characteristics of a resilient workforce:

- **Adaptability and Flexibility:** The ability to learn new skills, adjust to changing work processes, and embrace new technologies is essential in a dynamic environment.

- **Problem-Solving Skills:** A resilient workforce can effectively analyze challenges, identify solutions, and implement them to overcome obstacles.

- **Communication and Collaboration:** Strong communication and collaboration skills allow employees to work effectively together, share information, and navigate challenges as a team.

- **Critical Thinking and Decision-Making:** The ability to analyze information, weigh options, and make sound decisions is crucial in situations requiring adaptation or unforeseen disruptions.

- **Stress Management and Resilience:** The ability to manage stress effectively and remain calm under pressure is important for maintaining focus and productivity during challenging times.

- **Growth Mindset:** A growth mindset encourages employees to view challenges as opportunities for learning and development. This fosters a culture of continuous improvement and resilience in the face of change. Employees with a growth mindset believe their skills and abilities can be developed through effort and practice, making them more adaptable and willing to embrace new technologies or processes.

Strategies for Building a Resilient Workforce: Empowering Your People

Building a resilient workforce requires a multi-pronged approach:

- **Skills Development and Training:** Invest in training programs to equip your employees with the skills they need to adapt to technological advancements, changing consumer demands, and evolving regulations.

- **Cross-Training Opportunities:** Encourage cross-training opportunities that allow employees to gain experience in different areas and become more versatile within their roles.

- **Empowerment and Ownership:** Empower your employees by giving them ownership over their tasks and encouraging them to take initiative. This fosters a sense of responsibility and engagement, leading to a more resilient workforce.

- **Open Communication and Transparency:** Maintain open communication channels and keep employees informed about changes, challenges, and upcoming developments. Transparency fosters trust and allows employees to feel prepared for potential disruptions.

- **A Culture of Continuous Learning:** Foster a culture of continuous learning within your organization by encouraging employees to learn new skills, participate in professional development opportunities, and stay abreast of industry trends.

- **Employee Well-being Programs:** Invest in employee well-being programs that promote physical and mental health. A healthy and well-rested workforce is better equipped to handle challenges and adapt to change.

- **Mentorship Programs:** Implement both formal and informal mentorship programs. Formal programs pair experienced employees with new hires for guidance and career development. These programs can be structured with specific goals and timelines, providing a clear framework for mentorship. Informal mentorship can occur organically within teams, allowing senior colleagues to share knowledge and provide support to junior colleagues. Mentorship benefits both parties; mentors gain leadership experience by coaching and developing others, while mentees acquire valuable knowledge and insights from experienced colleagues.

- **Scenario Planning:** Conduct scenario planning exercises to prepare for potential disruptions. This involves brainstorming various future scenarios, such as a natural disaster or a cyberattack, and developing contingency plans to address them. By anticipating potential challenges, companies can build a more resilient workforce that can react effectively when disruptions occur. Scenario planning workshops can be facilitated internally or with the help of external consultants. This process encourages creative thinking and helps identify potential weaknesses in current operations. Developing contingency plans allows companies to be better prepared to respond to unforeseen disruptions and minimize negative impacts on the business.

- **Diversity and Inclusion:** Fostering diversity and inclusion within the workforce can significantly contribute to building resilience. Teams with a variety of backgrounds, experiences, and perspectives are better equipped to approach challenges creatively and find innovative solutions. An inclusive environment where employees feel comfortable sharing ideas leads to more effective problem-solving and better decision-making in the face of change. A diverse workforce can identify potential blind spots and bring a wider range of perspectives to the table, leading to more comprehensive solutions during challenging times.

The Role of Leadership in Building Resilience

Leadership plays a critical role in fostering a resilient workforce:

- **Leading by Example:** Leaders must demonstrate a commitment to learning, adaptability, and problem-solving, setting the tone for the entire organization.

- **Communicating the Vision:** Clearly communicate the company's vision and how it aligns with adapting to change and ensuring business continuity.

- **Building Trust and Psychological Safety:** Create a work environment where employees feel encouraged to share ideas, voice concerns, and take calculated risks without fear of reprimand.

- **Providing Coaching and Mentorship:** Offer coaching and mentorship opportunities to help employees develop the skills and confidence necessary to navigate change and overcome challenges.

- **Recognizing and Rewarding Resilience:** Recognize and reward employees who demonstrate adaptability, problem-solving skills, and a positive attitude in the face of change.

Building Resilience Through Effective Change Management:

Successfully navigating change is a key aspect of building a resilient workforce:

- **Clear Communication:** Clearly communicate the reasons for change, the anticipated outcomes, and the timeline for implementation.

- **Employee Involvement:** Involve employees in the change process whenever possible. This can be achieved by soliciting feedback, addressing concerns, and offering opportunities for input on implementation strategies.

- **Training and Support:** Provide employees with the necessary training and support to adapt to changes. This could include technical training for new technologies, process training for new workflows, or communication skills training for navigating difficult conversations during change implementation.

- **Change Management Champions:** Identify and empower change champions within your workforce. These individuals can act as advocates for change, answer questions from colleagues, and provide peer-to-peer support during the transition process.

- **Celebrating Milestones:** Celebrate milestones and successes achieved throughout the change process. Recognizing progress helps maintain employee morale and keeps them engaged in the change journey.

The Future of Work in Food Manufacturing: Embracing Disruption as an Opportunity

The food manufacturing industry is on the cusp of significant transformation. By developing a resilient workforce that is adaptable, skilled, and prepared to embrace change, food manufacturers can not only navigate disruptions but also thrive in a dynamic and evolving marketplace. Resilient workforces are better equipped to:

- **Drive Innovation:** A culture of continuous learning and problem-solving fosters innovation, allowing companies to develop new products, processes, and business models to meet changing consumer demands.

- **Enhance Efficiency and Productivity:** A resilient workforce can readily adapt to new technologies and optimize workflows, leading to increased efficiency and productivity within the manufacturing process.

- **Maintain Business Continuity:** In the face of unforeseen disruptions, a resilient workforce can quickly adapt, find solutions, and minimize the impact on operations, ensuring business continuity.

- **Attract and Retain Top Talent:** A company known for its commitment to employee development, adaptability, and a culture of resilience will be more attractive to top talent seeking a future-proof career path.

Building a resilient workforce requires ongoing effort and investment. However, the benefits are substantial. A workforce equipped with the skills, knowledge, and mindset to adapt to change and embrace new opportunities is vital for ensuring long-term success in the ever-evolving food manufacturing landscape. By prioritizing resilience, food manufacturers can position themselves not only to weather disruptions but also to become leaders in an industry poised for significant transformation.

CHAPTER 11

The Future of Food Manufacturing: A Tapestry of Innovation, Sustainability, and Resilience

The food manufacturing industry stands at a crossroads. Consumer preferences are evolving rapidly, technological advancements are transforming production processes, and environmental concerns necessitate a shift towards sustainable practices. This concluding chapter provides a comprehensive overview of the key themes explored throughout this book, weaving them together to create a vision for the future of food manufacturing: a tapestry of innovation, sustainability, and resilience.

A Recap of Key Themes:

- **Chapter 1: Introduction:** We explored the fundamental role food manufacturing plays in nourishing the global population and the complex challenges and opportunities that lie ahead.

- **Chapter 2: Understanding Consumer Trends:** A deep dive into evolving consumer demands, with a focus on health and wellness, convenience, sustainability, and transparency.

- **Chapter 3: Building a Strong Brand Identity:** The importance of crafting a compelling brand identity that resonates with consumers and differentiates your company within the marketplace.

- **Chapter 4: Innovation Through Product Development:** Strategies for innovation in product development, emphasizing the importance of research and development (R&D), market research, and staying ahead of consumer trends.

- **Chapter 5: Optimizing Production Processes:** Exploring techniques for optimizing production processes for efficiency, quality control, and cost reduction.

- **Chapter 6: Ensuring Food Safety:** The paramount importance of food safety throughout the entire food manufacturing lifecycle, from sourcing ingredients to product packaging and distribution.

- **Chapter 7: Building Your Value Proposition:** Crafting a compelling value proposition that attracts and retains top talent in a competitive job market. (We also explored employer branding strategies and measuring the ROI of your value proposition in Part 2.)

- **Chapter 8: Embracing Technological Advancements:** The transformative impact of automation, robotics, artificial intelligence (AI), big data, and the Internet of Things (IoT) on the food manufacturing industry.

- **Chapter 9: Sustainability in Food Manufacturing:** Strategies for adopting sustainable practices throughout the production process, minimizing environmental impact, and contributing to a healthier planet.

- **Chapter 10: Building a Resilient Food Manufacturing Workforce:** Developing a workforce with the skills, knowledge, and adaptability to navigate change and ensure business continuity in a dynamic environment.

Emerging Trends Shaping the Future:

Beyond the themes explored in the preceding chapters, here are some additional trends poised to shape the future of food manufacturing:

- **Personalized Nutrition:** The rise of personalized nutrition solutions tailored to individual health needs and preferences presents an opportunity for food manufacturers to develop new product lines or partner with nutrition technology companies. However, navigating data privacy concerns and ensuring the accessibility of personalized nutrition solutions will be crucial for long-term success.

- **Cellular Agriculture:** Cellular agriculture, also known as lab-grown meat, has the potential to revolutionize protein production and address sustainability concerns in the meat industry. While technological advancements are ongoing, regulatory frameworks and consumer acceptance will be key factors influencing the future of this technology.

- **Vertical Farming:** The growing adoption of vertical farming techniques allows for cultivating crops indoors with minimal environmental impact and improved resource efficiency. However, the initial investment costs associated with setting up vertical farming facilities can be a challenge.

- **Food Waste Reduction:** Increased focus on innovative solutions to minimize food waste throughout the supply chain, including upcycling technologies and improved forecasting methods, is essential for a sustainable food system. Collaboration between governments, businesses, and consumers will be crucial to achieve significant reductions in food waste.

- **The Rise of E-commerce:** The growing influence of e-commerce platforms in food retail requires food manufacturers to adapt their packaging and distribution strategies to cater to online grocery shopping. Investing in e-commerce fulfillment capabilities and ensuring product quality during transport will be essential for success in this growing market.

Weaving Innovation, Sustainability, and Resilience:

The future of food manufacturing lies in weaving together the threads of innovation, sustainability, and resilience. Innovation is essential to develop new products and processes that meet evolving consumer demands. Sustainability practices ensure environmental responsibility and resource conservation for future generations. A resilient workforce is vital to adapt to technological advancements, navigate disruptions, and ensure business continuity.

Conclusion

The journey towards a thriving future in food manufacturing necessitates embracing these interconnected themes. By fostering a culture of innovation, prioritizing sustainability, and developing a resilient workforce, food manufacturers can not only survive but also thrive in a dynamic and ever-changing landscape. This book has equipped you with the knowledge and strategies to navigate these challenges and contribute to a future of food manufacturing that is not only innovative and efficient but also environmentally responsible and socially conscious.

Embrace the Future of Food Manufacturing

The future of food manufacturing is bright, but it requires a proactive approach. By embracing innovation, prioritizing sustainability, and developing a resilient workforce, you can position your company for long-term success. Use the knowledge and strategies outlined in this book to navigate the evolving food manufacturing landscape and contribute to a future that nourishes both people and the planet.

CHAPTER 12

A Roadmap for Success: Putting the Pieces Together

The future of food manufacturing is bright, but the road to success requires careful planning, strategic execution, and continuous adaptation. Building upon the foundational concepts explored throughout this book, Chapter 12 provides a comprehensive roadmap for navigating the complexities of the food manufacturing industry and achieving long-term success. This roadmap outlines key considerations and actionable steps across various aspects of your business, empowering you to chart a course towards a thriving future.

1. Understanding Your Market and Your Competitive Landscape

- **Conduct thorough market research:** Analyze consumer trends, identify emerging market segments, and assess the competitive landscape. Understanding your target audience and their evolving needs is crucial for developing successful products and strategies.

- **Define your competitive advantage:** What sets your company apart from the competition? Is it your focus on innovation, your commitment to sustainability, or your dedication to high-quality ingredients? Clearly articulate your unique selling proposition (USP) to resonate with consumers and differentiate yourself within the marketplace.

- **Benchmarking:** Regularly benchmark your performance against industry leaders to identify areas for improvement and stay ahead of the curve.

2. Building a Strong Brand Identity

- **Develop a compelling brand story:** Craft a narrative that captures the essence of your company, its values, and its commitment to providing high-quality food products.

- **Invest in brand consistency:** Maintain a consistent brand identity across all communication channels, from your website and packaging to your social media presence and marketing materials.

- **Leverage the power of storytelling:** Consumers connect with stories. Share the stories behind your ingredients, your production processes, and the people who make your products.

3. Innovation Through Product Development

- **Establish a culture of innovation:** Foster a culture that encourages creativity, experimentation, and out-of-the-box thinking within your product development team.

- **Invest in research and development (R&D):** Dedicating resources to R&D allows you to explore new technologies, ingredients, and product formulations to stay ahead of the curve and meet evolving consumer demands.

- **Embrace open innovation:** Consider collaborating with universities, research institutions, or even startup companies to leverage their expertise and accelerate innovation.

4. Optimizing Production Processes for Efficiency and Quality

- **Continuous improvement:** Embrace a continuous improvement philosophy, constantly seeking ways to optimize your production processes, minimize waste, and improve efficiency.

- **Invest in automation and technology:** Identify opportunities to leverage automation and technology to streamline processes, enhance consistency, and reduce manual labor costs.

- **Implement robust quality control measures:** Establish and maintain rigorous quality control procedures throughout your production process to ensure product safety and consistency.

5. Building a Culture of Food Safety

- **Develop a comprehensive food safety plan:** Implement a Hazard Analysis and Critical Control Points (HACCP) plan and adhere to all food safety regulations to ensure the safety of your products.

- **Invest in employee training:** Provide ongoing food safety training for your employees to ensure they understand safe handling practices and adhere to all safety protocols.

- **Regular audits and inspections:** Conduct regular internal audits and inspections to identify and address any potential food safety risks proactively.

6. Building Your Workforce: Attracting and Retaining Top Talent

- **Craft a compelling value proposition:** Develop a strong value proposition that highlights your company culture, career development opportunities, and commitment to employee well-being.

- **Invest in a strong employer brand:** Showcase your company as a desirable workplace through a positive employer brand and active engagement on social media platforms.

- **Develop a robust talent acquisition strategy:** Implement a comprehensive approach to attracting top talent, including attending industry job fairs, utilizing online recruiting platforms, and fostering strong relationships with universities and technical schools.

- **Foster a Diverse and Inclusive Workplace:** Actively promote diversity and inclusion within your workforce. This can be achieved through targeted recruitment efforts, unconscious bias training, and creating an inclusive work environment where all employees feel valued and respected. A diverse workforce brings a wider range of perspectives and experiences to the table, leading to more creative problem-solving and innovation.

7. Embracing Technological Advancements

- **Identify your technology needs:** Carefully assess your specific needs and challenges to determine which technologies can offer the most significant benefits for your company.

- **Develop a technology implementation plan:** Create a well-defined plan for integrating new technologies into your existing infrastructure, including training programs for your workforce.

- **Partner with technology providers:** Collaborate with reputable technology providers who can offer expertise, support, and ongoing maintenance for the implemented technologies.

8. Sustainability in Food Manufacturing

- **Conduct a sustainability audit:** Assess your environmental impact by analyzing resource consumption, waste generation, and greenhouse gas emissions. This serves as a baseline for measuring progress.

- **Set clear sustainability goals:** Establish ambitious yet achievable sustainability goals aligned with your overall business objectives. Track your progress regularly and celebrate milestones to maintain momentum.

- **Source ingredients responsibly:** Partner with suppliers who prioritize sustainable agricultural practices and ethical sourcing throughout their supply chains.

9. Cultivating a Culture of Resilience

- **Embrace a growth mindset:** Foster a culture that encourages continuous learning, adaptability, and a willingness to embrace change.

- **Invest in scenario planning:** Develop contingency plans for potential disruptions, such as supply chain issues, natural disasters, or economic downturns. This proactive approach ensures your company can adapt and navigate unforeseen challenges effectively.

- **Empower your workforce:** Trust your employees to make decisions, take ownership of their roles, and contribute to problem-solving efforts. This fosters a sense of responsibility and engagement, leading to a more resilient workforce.

10. Building Strong Partnerships

- **Collaborate with suppliers:** Develop strong relationships with your suppliers to ensure a reliable supply chain, negotiate favorable pricing, and work towards shared sustainability goals.

- **Partner with industry organizations:** Participate in industry associations and attend industry events to connect with peers, share best practices, and stay informed about the latest trends and regulations.

- **Forge strategic partnerships:** Explore strategic partnerships with complementary businesses to leverage expertise, expand your product portfolio, or access new markets.

11. Building a Data-Driven Culture

- **Invest in data collection and analysis tools:** Implement systems and tools to collect and analyze data across all aspects of your business operations.

- **Leverage data insights:** Turn data into actionable insights to inform decision-making, optimize processes, and identify areas for improvement.

- **Develop a data-driven culture:** Encourage a culture where data is valued and utilized to make informed decisions for greater efficiency and profitability.

12. Continuous Improvement: A Never-Ending Journey

The food manufacturing industry is dynamic, and success requires continuous improvement. Here are some key strategies:

- **Regularly review and assess your performance:** Evaluate your progress against established goals and identify areas where you can improve.

- **Embrace a culture of feedback:** Encourage open communication and actively seek feedback from employees, customers, and partners. This feedback allows you to identify blind spots and make necessary adjustments.

- **Stay informed about industry trends:** Continuously monitor industry trends, regulatory changes, and emerging technologies to ensure your company stays ahead of the curve.

The roadmap for success in food manufacturing is not a linear path, but rather a continuous journey of adaptation, innovation, and progress. By following the strategies outlined in this chapter and tailoring them to your specific context, you can chart a course towards a thriving future for your company. Remember, the key to success lies in your commitment to excellence, your ability to embrace change, and your dedication to building a sustainable and resilient future for your industry and the communities you serve.

Resources

The food manufacturing industry is undergoing a period of significant transformation. This Resources section equips you with valuable tools and platforms to stay informed about the latest trends, emerging technologies, and best practices that will shape the future of food. Navigate these resources to delve deeper into specific topics and gain a competitive edge in the ever-evolving food manufacturing landscape.

Industry Associations:

- **The National Food Processors Association (NFPA):** The NFPA is a leading advocate for the food and beverage processing industry, providing its members with resources, education, and industry representation. (https://www.nfpa-food.org/)

- **The Grocery Manufacturers Association (GMA):** The GMA represents the world's leading food, beverage, and consumer product companies, offering its members guidance on industry trends, consumer insights, and public policy issues. (https://www.gmabrands.com/)

- **The Institute of Food Technologists (IFT):** The IFT is a global organization of food science and technology professionals, providing its members with access to scientific research, networking opportunities, and professional development resources. (https://www.ift.org/)

- **The Food Safety Preventive Controls Alliance (FSPCA):** The FSPCA is a public-private partnership focused on building capacity and collaboration for food safety within the food industry. (https://www.fspca.net/)

Publications and Periodicals:

- **Food Processing Magazine:** A leading publication covering the food and beverage processing industry, featuring articles on new technologies, processing techniques, and industry trends. (https://www.foodprocessing.com/)

- **Food Technology Magazine:** The official publication of the Institute of Food Technologists, featuring articles on scientific advancements, research findings, and applications of food science in the food industry. (https://www.ift.org/)

- **Prepared Foods Magazine:** A publication focused on the prepared foods industry, offering insights on product development, consumer trends, and food safety regulations. (https://www.preparedfoods.com/)

- **Food Engineering Magazine:** A publication dedicated to the engineering and design aspects of food manufacturing, featuring articles on automation, processing equipment, and plant operations. (https://www.foodengineeringmag.com/)

Online Resources:

- **U.S. Food and Drug Administration (FDA) Food Safety Resources:** The FDA website provides a comprehensive collection of resources on food safety regulations, compliance requirements, and best practices for food manufacturers. (https://www.fda.gov/food/retail-food-protection/fda-food-code)

- **The United Nations Food and Agriculture Organization (FAO) Food and Agriculture Industry Division:** The FAO website offers valuable resources on sustainable food production practices, global food security challenges, and technological advancements shaping the future of food. (https://www.fao.org/home/en)

- **The International Food Information Service (IFIS):** The IFIS database provides access to scientific research, technical reports, and market data on a wide range of food science and technology topics. (https://www.ifis.org/)

www.ingramcontent.com/pod-product-compliance
Lightning Source LLC
LaVergne TN
LVHW051035070526
838201LV00009B/207